CARLSON'S MARINE RAIDERS

Makin Island 1942

GORDON L. ROTTMAN

First published in Great Britain in 2014 by Osprey Publishing,
PO Box 883, Oxford, OX1 9PL, UK
PO Box 3985, New York, NY 10185-3985, USA
E-mail: info@ospreypublishing.com

Osprey Publishing is part of the Osprey Group

A CIP catalog record for this book is available from the British Library

Print ISBN: 978 1 4728 0327 6
PDF ebook ISBN: 978 1 4728 0328 3
ePub ebook ISBN: 978 1 4728 0329 0

Index by Alan Rutter
Typeset in Sabon
Maps by bounford.com
3D BEVs by Alan Gilliland
Originated by PDQ Media, Bungay, UK
Printed in China through Worldprint Ltd

14 15 16 17 18   10 9 8 7 6 5 4 3 2 1

Osprey Publishing is supporting the Woodland Trust, the UK's leading woodland conservation charity, by funding the dedication of trees.

www.ospreypublishing.com

ACKNOWLEDGEMENTS

The author appreciates Tom Laemlein of Armor Plate Press for his photographic support and Ken Haney for the loan of photographs and his advice. The US Marine Corps Historical Center was especially helpful with much assistance provided by Charles Melson (chief historian), Annette Amerman (senior historian), and Kara Newcomer (photo historian). Thanks also to James Ginther and John Kull of the Defense Prisoner of War/Missing Personnel Office and George Kum Kee and Tiuti Biribo of the Kiribati Tourism Office for the photos they provided by Dennis Pack. Much thanks also goes to Akira "Taki" Takizawa for his input.

ARTISTS' NOTE

Readers may care to note that the original paintings from which the color plates of this book were prepared are available for private sale. All reproduction copyright whatsoever is retained by the Publishers. The Publishers regret that they can enter into no correspondence upon this matter.

Inquiries regarding the battlescene painting should be addressed to Johnny Shumate (shumate1977@gmail.com), and inquiries regarding the cover painting to Mark Stacey (mark@mrstacey.plus.com).

US MARINE CORPS RANKS

Pvt	Private
FM1c	Field Music 1st Class
PFC	Private 1st Class
Corp	Corporal
Sgt	Sergeant
PlSgt	Platoon Sergeant
GySgt	Gunnery Sergeant
MGySgt	Master Gunnery Sergeant
1stSgt	1st Sergeant
SgtMaj	Sergeant Major
2dLt	2d Lieutenant
1stLt	1st Lieutenant
Capt	Captain
Maj	Major
LtCol	Lieutenant Colonel
Col	Colonel
BrigGen	Brigadier General ("one-star")
MajGen	Major General ("two-star")
LtGen	Lieutenant General ("three-star")

CONTENTS

INTRODUCTION

In the summer of 1942, the United States was battling to reverse the tide of the Pacific War. In the few months since the Japanese attack on Pearl Harbor, the nation had taken further staggering blows with the loss of Guam and Wake Island, the humiliating fall of the Philippines in April 1942, and the surrender of Corregidor Island in May. The British Commonwealth had suffered its own equally disastrous setbacks throughout the region, and the Dutch East Indies, with its vast natural resources, had fallen under Japanese control. The Japanese conquest did not reach its fullest extent until August 1942.

The road back would be difficult, and every opportunity to inflict damage on the all-conquering Japanese had to be taken. On April 18, 1942, the Doolittle bomber raid on Tokyo was launched, inflicting little real damage, but proving to be a tremendous morale boost to the American people. Even before the Philippines fell, American defense forces began occupying South Pacific islands not yet seized by the Japanese.

The Japanese had originally planned to continue their conquest across the South Pacific. Their strategy was to first take Midway in early June, and then in August move on Fiji, New Caledonia, and Samoa – all defended by Allied forces, mostly American – in hopes of cutting the supply line between Hawaii and Australia and New Zealand. The Imperial Japanese Navy (IJN) suffered the disastrous loss of four aircraft carriers during the June 4–5 battle of Midway, which led to the cancellation of the more ambitious plans on July 11. Though at the time it was not fully realized how vital it was, the US Navy's victory at Midway allowed the Allies to begin launching offensive operations. The Australians began to fight back on Papua and New Guinea the following month, and US forces were ready to take the fight to the Japanese too.

The Japanese had quietly moved into the lower Solomons at the beginning of May 1942, extending their reach towards eastern Australia. They had occupied Buka, Bougainville, and the Shortland Islands in the upper

DECEMBER 7, 1941

Japanese attack Pearl Harbor, sparking the Pacific War

Solomons in March, establishing airfields and an advance naval base. Construction of an airfield on Guadalcanal began in mid-June, from which the Japanese could threaten the sea routes between the US and the cities on Australia's east coast. It was discovered by American photoreconnaissance on July 4, was quickly bombed, and an amphibious landing, Operation *Watchtower*, was immediately ordered. The 1st Marine Division in New Zealand was dispatched to seize and hold all Japanese installations on Guadalcanal and Tulagi-Gavutu.

The first American amphibious assault since 1898 commenced in the pre-dawn hours of August 7, taking the Japanese completely by surprise. But it would be a long campaign. To support the ongoing operation, a diversion was planned to distract the Japanese and hopefully divert reinforcements to a small, out-of-the-way island 1,100 miles northwest of Guadalcanal and 2,000 miles southwest of Pearl Harbor.

This small joint Navy and Marine operation had another objective, perhaps more important than the tactical mission: to provide a morale boost to the home front in the same manner as the Doolittle Raid four and a half months earlier. This operation, the first of its kind – an amphibious raid delivered by submarine after an extremely long-range infiltration through hostile waters – would be executed by a special unit. The raid would also publicly showcase the capabilities of these troops, the Marine Raiders – a new commando-style unit raised just weeks after the bombing of Pearl Harbor, with the intention of taking the war to the enemy.

Compared to most battles of World War II, the Makin Island raid was only a skirmish, involving just over a couple hundred US Marines, less than a hundred Japanese Navy shore personnel, two US submarines, a few dozen Japanese aircraft, and two small Japanese auxiliary vessels. But its repercussions were out of proportion to the forces involved. The target date was August 17, ten days after the Guadalcanal landing.

Lieutenant Colonel Evans F. Carlson (left front) consults a map with his officers when the 2nd Raider Bn was training at Camp Elliot, California, spring 1942. Evans Carlson was a controversial and eccentric commander for the Makin operation, which resulted in a questionable outcome with tragic and possibly avoidable losses. (Tom Laemlein/Armor Plate Press)

ORIGINS

Raiders from out of the sea

After the fall of France and the evacuation of Dunkirk in 1940, Britain was left incapable of mounting any major amphibious operations in Europe. But, needing to continue the fight somehow, it started raising units of amphibious special troops – the Commandos – whose purpose was to keep the Germans off balance as the British Army rebuilt. With war in the Pacific looming, in 1941–42 several Marine officers and NCOs observed or undertook British Commando and amphibious-assault training, as did Army officers.

But in the US armed forces, the job of amphibious raiding had traditionally belonged to the Marine Corps, and in 1938 the Marines had in fact already experimented with rubber boats to land small raiding forces. The 1st Battalions of the 5th and 6th Marines were trained as "rubber-boat battalions" for this role. Exercises proved the concept viable. Scouts using rubber boats successfully reconnoitered landing beaches, but they were hampered at the time by the lack of compact man-portable radios to report timely intelligence to the yet-to-arrive landing force.

Evans Carlson

Two officers – Marine LtCol Evans F. Carlson and Army Col William J. Donovan, who both observed Commando training in 1941, separately encouraged the development of Marine units capable of waging what was called "guerrilla warfare," which was at the time a general term for covert behind-the-lines special operations. The proposed units would use guerrilla tactics and techniques such as ambushes, hit-and-run raids, and sabotage, while avoiding decisive engagements with superior forces.

Carlson was considered somewhat of a renegade within the Marine Corps. He had served as an observer with the Chinese in their war against Japan in 1937–38 and 1940, and was impressed by their hit-and-run tactics against a superior enemy, as well as their leadership style and organizational concepts. Since he promoted concepts endorsed by communists, he was considered somewhat suspect in the staunchly conservative Marine Corps, and his ideas would most likely have been ignored if it were not that one of his adherents was Marine Capt James "Jimmy" Roosevelt, the President's son. Also influencing the President was his friend and advisor Col Donovan (later to command the Office of Strategic Services), who recommended a similar concept based on his experiences observing British Commandos. Churchill too encouraged Roosevelt to consider using such units.

The Marine Corps split into two schools. Many, led by MajGen Holland Smith (then commanding the Atlantic Fleet Amphibious Corps) opposed the organization of specialized amphibious raider units, maintaining that all Marine units were capable of such operations by nature of their training. The other school – including Evans Carlson, and encouraged by President Roosevelt and Secretary of the Navy Frank Knox – felt that there was a specialist role for such units.

But senior officers, including the Commandant of the Marine Corps, MajGen Thomas Holcomb, were also wary of Col Donovan and his proposal to raise a commando force outside the purview of the Army or Navy/Marines, answering only to the Joint Chiefs of Staff. The fear was that such a unit risked eroding the Marine Corps' identity and would lead to it eventually being absorbed into the Army. With the President supporting the idea and the Army considering it, the Marine Corps thought it would be prudent to raise such units. Besides, there just might be a use for them. With the President's urging, the Marine Corps reluctantly complied; in January 1942 Admiral Ernest King ordered the activation of two Marine commando-type units.

Amphibious experiments

Although opposed to the creation of separate Marine Raider units, MajGen Smith did endorse the concept of the Marines being able to land a light strike force via rubber boats. This concept underwent further testing during Fleet

The USS *Nautilus* conducting a rubber-boat exercise at Dutch Harbor, Unalaska Island in the Aleutians. The troops are probably from the Army's 7th Provisional Scout Battalion rehearsing for the May 1943 Attu Island assault. (US Marine Historical Center)

EVANS F. CARLSON'S EARLY CAREER

Born in Sidney, New York on February 26, 1896, Evans Carlson was raised in Massachusetts and Vermont, his father a minister. He ran away from home at 11, but returned. In 1910 he did it again and did not return. He later joined the Army as an artilleryman at age 16, when 21 was the minimum age. After serving in the Philippines and Hawaii, he was discharged in 1915 as an assistant sergeant major, at only 19 years old. Assigned to the Reserves, he was recalled in 1916 after marrying Dorothy Seccombe. Assigned as an artillery instructor in Texas, the following year he was commissioned into the regular Army field artillery as a 2nd lieutenant. Four months later he was a 1st lieutenant, and early the next year was promoted to captain. He wrote to his father regarding his concept of leadership:

"I love my men but I must keep them working. When the work is over, I must see that they have some recreation. I must always see that they have sufficient food and shelter wherever it is possible. I will lead a man, if he will be led. But I'll get him where he's got to go, even if I have to drive him. I never ask a man to do something I won't do myself. But I must never become too intimate with the men. An officer can mix with his men and show them that he does not feel himself above them, but still keeps a certain reserve."

Carlson and the 87th Division's 334th Field Artillery were shipped to France in time for the Armistice. Reluctant to leave France, he was assigned to Pershing's staff to investigate Medal of Honor recommendations. He resigned in 1919 and worked as a produce salesman for the California Packing Corporation.

Unhappy and divorced, he enlisted in the Marine Corps as a private in 1922 at age 26 and set straight his actual age in his records. Within days he was a corporal, and was soon assigned to the Basic School for officer training. At the end of the year he was commissioned a 2nd lieutenant and assigned to the 5th Marines. He married Estelle Sawyer in 1924. Carlson began aviator training that same year, which he failed. After that he guarded mail trains after a rash of robberies swept through the country. In February 1927, assigned to the 4th Marines, he arrived in China for an international security mission. He remained in China as an intelligence officer until 1929. Carlson was assigned to the Marine-led Guardia Nacional in Nicaragua in 1930 as a Guardia captain leading a small detachment. He experienced his first combat in 18 years of service on a jungle patrol, which resulted in the award of the Navy Cross (the second highest decoration for valor). He next served as the Department Commander of Managua and later Chief of Police, receiving citations and Nicaraguan decorations. Coming back to the US in 1933, he soon returned to China as the 4th Marines' intelligence officer. In 1935 he once more came back to the US, where he became a general's aide. As second-in-command of President Roosevelt's guard at his Warm Springs, Georgia retreat, Carlson developed a friendship with the Commander-in-Chief. He furthered his education at George Washington University, becoming known as something of an intellectual, and reinforced his reputation for being outspoken.

The year 1937 found him in China studying Chinese. Before departing, President Roosevelt personally asked him to send reports on events in China. On arriving there, he found Japan locked in war with the Nationalist Chinese,

Landing Exercise Number 7 (FLEX 7) in February 1941, when Co A, E, and I, 7th Marines (one company per battalion) were reorganized as "provisional rubber-boat companies" and collectively called the Mobile Landing Group. The regiment was part of the just-activated 1st MarDiv located at Guantánamo Bay, Cuba. The companies were landed by rubber boat from three destroyer transports (APDs).[1] They executed divisionary operations and seized inland objectives to block enemy reinforcements approaching the main landing's beachhead.

During 1941 maneuvers in North Carolina, MajGen Smith employed 1st Bn, 5th Marines in a similar manner. Embarked aboard six APDs, the "light battalion" or "APD battalion" landed in the "enemy's" rear, along with attached parachute and tank companies, to attack the defenders' reserves

JANUARY 1942

Two Marine commando battalions ordered established

1 APDs were either World War I-era destroyers or newer destroyer escorts converted to high-speed (24 knots) troop transports capable of carrying 140 or 162 troops, respectively, and were often used to deliver raiders and scouts in the Pacific Theater. Their classification is from 'AP' for transport and 'D' for destroyer.

and the Chinese Red Army had completed its brutal Long March into northwest China. The Marco Polo Bridge Incident edged the country into total war. Carlson was reassigned as a naval attaché (observer) to learn how the Japanese fought. After hearing about the exploits of the Red Army and Mao Tse-tung, Carlson convinced Chiang Kai-shek to allow him to travel north and join up with the Red Army. He traveled thousands of miles with the Eighth Route Army, met with many communist leaders, and became enamored with their tactics and military philosophy. It was here that he heard the phrase "Gung Ho" (*gōng hé*), which means to work together in harmony.[2] After spending January to August 1938 with the Red Army, Carlson returned to the US at the end of 1938, and in April 1939 resigned his commission in order to publicly write and inform Americans of the real situation in China, warning that Japan was a serious threat. He refused retirement, assignment to the Reserve, or promotion to major. He felt that he had no right to live off a military retirement while condemning some of the US's policies. From the end of 1938 he had written articles, given lectures, and written the books *The Chinese Army* and *Twin Stars of China*. Carlson returned to China in August 1940 and traveled the country, visiting government officials, businessmen, and collectives. He had separated from his second wife, and the divorce was finalized in 1943. He departed China in January 1941 to report his findings to the President, State Department, and Navy Department. He briefed Field Marshal MacArthur in Manila, but the Military Advisor to the Commonwealth Government was not attracted to Carlson's unorthodox ideas and had no interest in preparing the Philippine Army for jungle combat, much less guerrilla warfare. Carlson continued to lecture and give interviews, predicting war with Japan within months. In April 1941 he received a Marine Reserve major's commission. He could not be granted a Regular commission as he had resigned. He soon began lobbying for the creation of a commando-type unit and was sent to Britain to observe Commando training.

(US Marine Historical Center)

2 Linguist Gerald L. Cohen, of the University of Missouri-Rolla, offers the theory that "Gung Ho" does not mean "work together" in Mandarin but was the clipped form of the term *Gongye Hezhoushe* – Industrial Cooperative – based on the first syllable of each word. "Work together" in colloquial Mandarin may be *gongtong nuli*.

and block their lines of communications. It was proposed that the battalion be reorganized into four small rifle companies, each with a headquarters and a weapons company and armed with light weapons. A division of six APDs could carry the six companies, their size restricted by the 140 troops the early APDs could transport. The Marines could not afford to make 1st Bn, 5th Marines a separate unit as additional troops to raise a new battalion for the regiment were unavailable. But Pearl Harbor changed this.

A role for the Raiders

The earlier concepts had envisioned raiders directly supporting the main amphibious assault. But in early 1942 the idea of raiders operating independently against the Japanese now seemed viable. Like the British, who formed the Commandos after suffering early defeats, America too needed a means of fighting back for morale purposes and to gain time to rebuild. A unit capable of executing economy-of-force raids seemed to meet the requirement – lightning-fast amphibious raids to harass the enemy, tie down their forces for coastal defense, and destroy installations and materiel. Like the Commandos and Army Rangers, the Marine Raiders would be light, amphibious strike units well-suited for operations in the Pacific. The first were designated "separate battalions" along the lines of the early Australian commando companies referred to as "independent companies."

The 1st Separate Bn was organized from 1st Bn, 5th Marines, 1st MarDiv at Quantico, Virginia on January 6, 1942 with LtCol Merritt A. "Red Mike" Edson commanding. Because of the President's urging for such units, the Navy approved the formation of a second unit on January 23, 1942. On February 4 the 2nd MarDiv at San Diego activated the 2nd Separate Bn with LtCol Evans F. Carlson commanding and Capt James Roosevelt as XO – he was promoted to major in May.

At the suggestion of MajGen Charles F. B. Price, commanding 2nd MarDiv, the 1st and 2nd Separate Battalions were redesignated "Raider" on February 16 and 19, respectively. They were soon assigned to Amphibious Corps, Atlantic and Pacific Fleets, respectively. The proposed organization for the light battalions was adopted, although there were organizational and philosophical differences between the two battalions.

Six months after the Marines organized its first Raider battalion, the Army raised its first Ranger battalion. Eventually, the Army raised six Ranger battalions and the Marines four Raider battalions. All were organized in a similar way to a British Commando[3], and armed with the equivalent US weapons.

The "Gung Ho" philosophy

While newly raised units are referred to as "established" or "organized," the 2nd Raider Bn was "created" or perhaps "sculpted." It was unique among US military units, a bold yet questionable experiment that has never been replicated.

Carlson faced an uphill battle to raise his unit, but his unorthodox ideas on how to run the battalion met with even greater opposition. Carlson's concept was for a light, agile unit capable of striking Japanese-held islands swiftly, achieving complete surprise, to weaken their defenses prior to landing the main force. He intended to blend the tactics and techniques of the Commandos with those of the Chinese guerrillas. This aspect met with little opposition in the Corps, other than from those opponents who felt that specialized units were unnecessary.

What was difficult to accept was Carlson's "Gung Ho" concept of leadership and day-to-day unit routine, based on Chinese Communist principles. Carlson went so far as to propose that the distinctions between officers, NCOs, and enlisted men be abolished and that there should be only "leaders" and "fighters," the former having no special privileges. Initially many of the Raider officers and NCOs were opposed to this, or at least dubious. There was no compromise on Carlson's part. The Raider volunteers

3 The British term "commando," besides identifying a unit member, was the equivalent of a battalion – a single term defining its mission and size. A commando consisted of six "troops," which were small companies.

Carlson and Roosevelt plan training while the battalion is still in California. Note the Chippewa engineer boots, Blucher high-top boots, and moccasins under the field table. (US Marine Historical Center)

either accepted his concepts or were out. Some, though not accepting all his ideas, remained, keeping their thoughts to themselves.

No one wore rank insignia in the field. There were no separate messes and no one skipped to the head of the chow line. The leaders shared all the hardships and received no better treatment than the fighters. There was no saluting in the unit area, and officers were not addressed as "Sir." Liberty was limited, and the Raiders were segregated from other units. This, of course, instilled an inflated sense of superiority and led to problems with "other Marines." Leaders were selected by their ability to lead and not necessarily by seniority.

Carlson's philosophy was for a harmonious relationship between all ranks and elements within the unit. Teamwork was essential and took priority over the individual. One had to be responsible for one's actions, or inaction. What was difficult for many to grasp was the communist-style "self-criticism" sessions. After an exercise each man stood before his squad or platoon and assessed his actions and mistakes. They were also given the

LANDING CRAFT, RUBBER (LARGE)

Adopted in 1938, "rubber boats" were essential for Raiders and scouts to move from ship to shore. Since they were transported by submarines, PT boats, and other small craft where space was at a premium, deflated boats could be easily stowed. They could be inflated by two hand-operated pumps, but on submarines and surface craft compressed-air hoses were available. The 395lb LCR(L) was made of black synthetic rubber with three rubber bench seats supported by inflated tubes below them. They were sometimes painted with blue-gray rubber paint. The tubular hull measured 16ft in length with an 8ft beam, and was divided into ten separate cells, allowing the boat to maintain floatation with two-thirds of the cells punctured. It was designed for ten men, but 12 and even more could be carried. Ten short and two long wooden paddles (here not to scale) were provided as a quiet means of propulsion. The Evinrude 9.5hp, two-cylinder outboard motors were temperamental, unreliable, and too noisy for covert operations unless there was loud surf, as there was at Makin. They lacked engine cowlings that would have provided some silencing, and the coil and magneto were susceptible to seawater damage. The outboards gave the boat a speed of 3.5–4.5 knots, but most importantly provided enough power to push through surf. Accessories included a repair kit, wooden bullet-hole plugs, bailers, an emergency CO_2 inflation bottle, and a sea anchor.

opportunity to (mildly) criticize their immediate leaders. But this was still the Marines Corps and any Marine knew that their leaders had ways to make things tougher for them. Carlson's idea was to instill a sense of responsibility among all hands, a sense that they were accountable for the effectiveness of the unit and the well-being of all troops. He called this, "collective consensus and ethical conviction."

Instead of staffs developing plans that the troops would obediently carry out, "Gung Ho talks" were held at all echelons. The idea was that squads and platoons would have input into operational plans, and there would be "decentralized decision making." The troops would be able to propose options and their own ideas based on their experience. Reason, rather than authority, would be the basis for decision making, resulting in a "collective consensus." The troops had a stake in the plan and Carlson expected them to take their American citizenship seriously. There was even a degree of political indoctrination. He encouraged the men to think for themselves and not be mindless cannon fodder.

Of course, when engaged in combat the "Gung Ho talks" and group discussion was impossible. They had to respond to their leader's commands immediately and without question. Carlson's idealized leadership concepts and group input somewhat eroded proven military discipline. Opponents criticized his concepts as damaging both discipline and morale, and believed that there was no place for democracy in a military organization.

Carlson even insisted his Raiders follow the Chinese example of field rations. The "rice ration" or R-ration consisted of rice with raisins, a chunk of bacon, an onion, and sometimes a tasteless D-ration enriched chocolate bar that the Raiders cooked themselves. This was less than satisfactory, as eating a rice-based diet for prolonged periods was monotonous and not very palatable to Americans. The rice was not instant, so it required cooking for 20–40 minutes, plus the time taken to collect firewood and build a fire. Since

FEBRUARY 1942

Carlson's 2nd Marine Raiders activated

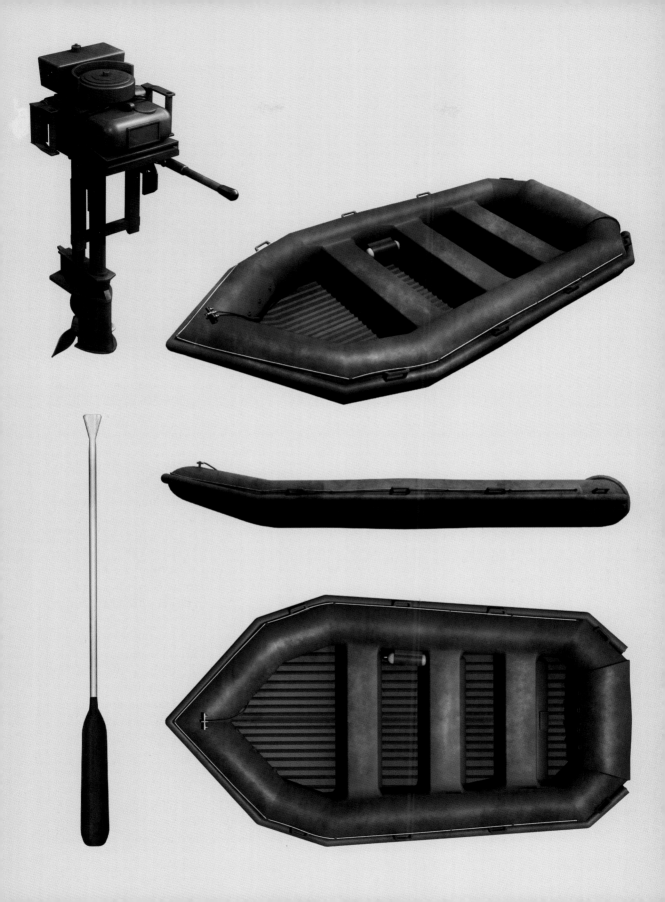

canteen cups had no lid to cover them while cooking, the rice was sticky. The bacon quickly went rancid. Of course, the preparation of such rations was impractical during multi-day operations requiring constant movement. The Raiders were expected to go without food for the planned one-day Makin raid, but when forced to remain another day they searched for food and asked natives for handouts.

A new kind of Marine battalion

At the tactical level, Carlson strove to create a self-contained, highly proficient unit that could fight outnumbered and win, operate on any terrain under any weather conditions, and move cross-country more rapidly than conventional units. They would not be reliant on field artillery or air support. Envisioned to be submarine-delivered, the limited fire support these craft could provide could not be counted on, as they had to submerge if there was an air threat. Submarines also provided a mobile floating base able to dispatch ammunition and supplies ashore, provide a communications relay, alert the infantry to incoming aircraft via radar and lookouts, and treat evacuated casualties. The troop-transport submarine had the advantage of being able to submerge for protection rather than be vulnerable to attack, as surface vessels were.

Carlson also felt that a Raider battalion would be able to conduct longer-duration inland operations to harass the enemy's rear area. This would demand guerrilla-style tactics, but still relied on an external resupply source; a roving military unit conducting aggressive operations could not live off the land or enjoy support from an indigenous population.

This concept was later proved viable, though difficult, during Carlson's epic 30-day "Long Patrol" on Guadalcanal and the 1st and 4th Raider Battalions' weeks-long operation on New Georgia.

Besides Carlson's philosophical theories, a Raider unit required at least four months of grueling training in more-grounded military subjects. Physical fitness was a primary requirement, and officers were expected to be able to do everything the enlisted men could. A forced march speed of 7mph was required, which demanding both walking and running (normal infantry walking speed is 4mph). Marches of 10–50 miles were common. Much effort was placed on cross-country infiltration tactics, with the "attainment of objectives by unorthodox and unexpected methods." This meant overland movement in all types of terrain and vegetation and included extensive land navigation, map reading, and compass experience. Unit runs, swimming, cliff climbing, boxing, hand-to-hand combat, knife and bayonet fighting, weapons training, demolitions, jungle craft, field hygiene, overcoming barbed-wire obstacles, and camouflage were all emphasized. Squad- and platoon-level tactics, infiltration courses, street fighting, ambushes, and patrolling were constantly practiced, especially at night. Training began at 0430 and lasted into the night, sometimes very late.

Carlson and Roosevelt personally interviewed volunteers from the 2nd MarDiv for men who could improvise, had outdoors experience, and sought adventure. The main goal of the interviews was to reject the rebels, troublemakers, and defiant loners. Teamwork was essential. All the interviewees were promised danger and hardship.

The 2nd Raiders was activated at Marine Corps Base, San Diego, California in February 1942. The 1st Raider Bn on the East Coast dispatched its partly trained Co A, a machine-gun platoon, and mortar section (197 troops in all) to the 2nd Battalion. Carlson rejected half of the officers and three-quarters of the men, which the 1st Bn commander, LtCol Merritt Edson, took as an insult, and for which he never forgave Carlson. Those selected were scattered through the 2nd Bn's four companies.

Waiting for a job

Carlson kept the President informed on the battalion's progress. Roosevelt gave assurances that they would soon be put to good use. By spring, higher commanders were concerned that both Raider battalions had been intensely trained to a high peak, and would lose their edge and morale would erode if not soon employed. The Pacific Fleet began to study possible missions. The 1st Raider Bn departed the US in April, and would be committed to the Guadalcanal operation, its first mission being a conventional amphibious assault on a small island.

The 2nd Raiders trained at Camp Elliot north of San Diego, quartered in the remote Jacques Farm (aka "Jack's Farm") to live in pup tents, eat from mess kits, suffer cold showers, and wash their clothes in buckets. They spent two weeks clearing and building their camp. From February they trained there for six weeks and in April undertook two weeks of rubber-boat training at San Clemente Island 70 miles off the California coast, launching

JAMES ROOSEVELT

The second child and first son of President Franklin D. Roosevelt was born in New York City on December 23, 1907. "Jimmy" Roosevelt attended schools in New York and Washington, DC, graduating from Gorton School in 1926 and Harvard in 1930. He was president of Roosevelt & Sargent, Inc., an insurance brokerage in Boston, Massachusetts. In 1936 President Roosevelt asked his son to accompany him to Argentina as his aide, and James was commissioned a Marine Corps Reserve lieutenant colonel without the benefit of any military experience. This drew a great deal of criticism, and in 1938 James put away the uniform to serve as his father's civilian administrative assistant. Criticism continued, labeling James as the "Assistant President" or "Crown Prince." He continued to perform as a Marine reservist, but felt guilty about his high rank, and he resigned in October 1939. He was involved with the movie industry from 1938–40. He rejoined the Reserves in November as a captain, attended the Company Officer School, and was assigned to a Reserve artillery battalion. He went on active duty in November 1940. In early 1941 the President sent James on a round-the-world trip informing various heads of state that the US would no doubt soon be in the war. In Crete and Iraq, James experienced German air attacks. Later in 1941 he served on Donovan's staff in what was then the Office of the Coordinator of Information, the fledging predecessor of the OSS.

He requested a combat assignment after the attack on Pearl Harbor. Aware of Carlson's idea for a commando unit, James helped promote it. When the 2nd Raider Bn was organized, Carlson asked James to be his XO. The 35-year-old "Jimmy" Roosevelt was an unlikely Raider. He had more business and diplomatic experience than military, had had part of his stomach removed, had poor eyesight, and had flat feet. After the Makin raid he was given leave and did not participate in the "Long Patrol" on Guadalcanal. In October 1942 he was promoted to lieutenant colonel and given command of the new 4th Raider Bn raised in California. He was invalided when the unit departed for the South Pacific in February 1943. In November 1943 he served as the Marine liaison officer accompanying the Army seizure of Makin. There he received the Silver Star, giving him the unique distinction of being decorated for valor by two different services in two separate operations over a year apart on the same island. He served in staff positions for the rest of his career. He was released from active duty as a colonel in

October 1945 and retired from the Reserves in October 1959 as a brigadier general.

He rejoined Roosevelt & Sargent and unsuccessfully ran for various political offices until elected a California Congressman, serving five terms from 1955–65. He was later a public relations consultant until his passing away on August 13, 1991. He was buried in Corona del Mar, California.

Roosevelt's decorations
- Navy Cross
- Silver Star
- American Defense Service Medal
- American Campaign Medal
- Asiatic-Pacific Campaign Medal with four service stars
- World War II Victory Medal
- Marine Corps Reserve Medal with bronze star
- Philippine Liberation Medal with service star

(US Marine Historical Center)

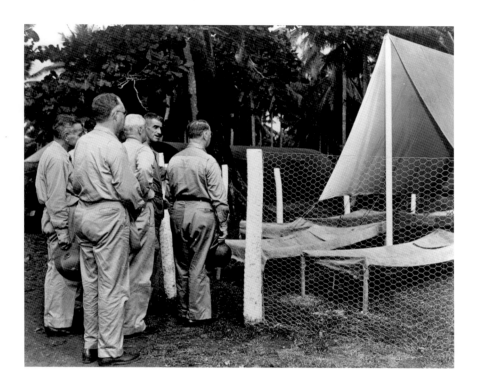

Carlson describes the makeshift field bivouac facilities his Raiders built at remote Jacques Farm on Camp Elliot. (US Marine Historical Center)

from destroyer transports. This included boarding and securing equipment, righting capsized boats, negotiating surf, speed-paddling, and operation and care of the temperamental outboard motors.

The battalion received all the top-notch equipment it needed, owing to Maj Roosevelt's name. While he strived to be just another Marine officer, he did not hesitate to use his influence to acquire the latest equipment, including the new "walkie-talkies," and the M1 semi-automatic rifles that the rest of the Corps would not see until later in the year.

In late March, Carlson was called to Hawaii to discuss his battalion's employment. A new emphasis on rubber-boat training occurred after his return. In mid-April two more companies were activated for 250 additional volunteers mixed with cadre leaders drawn from the original companies. Their training began immediately and continued until the battalion embarked aboard the troop transport USS *J. Franklin Bell* (AP34) on May 8 to arrive at a still-battered Pearl Harbor on May 18.

The Raiders set up home at Camp Catlin between Pearl Harbor and Honolulu. Training was stepped up and the new Co E and F – tagged "Junior Raiders" by the old hands – continued their initial training. On May 23, Co C and D departed to reinforce Midway Island under Maj Roosevelt for the expected battle. They saw no ground action except having to endure air raids. They rejoined the battalion on June 22. Forced marches over hills in a tropical climate increased, and a great deal of live-fire and tactical exercises were undertaken. In the six months from February to July 1942, Carlson's Raiders had turned into a lethal force. But then a new phase of training was about to commence for Co A and B.

SUMMER 1942

Planning begins for 2nd Raiders' first operation

INITIAL STRATEGY

Japan's "islands of mystery"

Makin Island, officially known as Butaritari, lies in the Gilbert Islands in the Central Pacific, an area where the Japanese had long had a presence. In 1914 a Japanese expeditionary force occupied German possessions in the Marshall, Caroline, and Mariana Islands. The League of Nations granted Japan a mandate to administer the former German possessions in 1920, which became known as the Japanese Mandate. Administered by the South Seas Bureau, the islands were economically exploited (in fishing, agriculture, and mining) and a resettlement program introduced Japanese settlers. All commercial activities fell under the control of the South Seas Development Company and the Nankai Trading Company.

By the late 1930s the Japanese population outnumbered the native. Japan withdrew from the League of Nations in 1935 and the Mandate became known as, in the phrases of the time, a "closed territory" and "Japan's islands of mystery." The US accused Japan of fortifying the islands. The 4th Fleet was established in 1939 to defend the Mandate – this was a local defense force rather than a conventional combat fleet, with few ships other than light forces. The fleet was headquartered at Truk, the "Japanese Pearl Harbor." Japan viewed the Marshall, Caroline, and Mariana Islands as the perfect outer defense for the Home Islands. Each of the three groups was provided a defense system centered on Jaluit, Truk, and Saipan, respectively. Other major bases were established at Kwajalein and Palau. While there were eventually some Imperial Japanese Army units assigned to the area, the Mandate was very much under the purview of the IJN.

To the south of the Marshalls was the British Gilbert and Ellice Crown Colony, established in 1916. In 1892 the region had been given British protectorate status in an effort to prevent exploitation of the natives by European traders. The Gilbert Islands consist of 16 coral atolls and islands of significance totaling 166 square miles. Some 700 miles to the southeast

are the Ellice Islands with nine atolls of only 14 square miles. The Gilberts would be occupied by the Japanese, but the Ellices, while abandoned by the British, were left untouched as they were too exposed to American attack from the Samoas and Fiji. The Ellices themselves would be occupied in stages by the US in October 1942 through August 1943.

The Gilbert and Ellice Crown Islands had been administered by a British resident commissioner on Ocean Island to the southwest, who governed through district commissioners and native magistrates overseeing the islands' fiscal, health, education, and legal systems. Australian trading firms handled the export of copra and phosphate. Much food was imported, but there was some subsistence farming and of course fishing. The Gilberts were divided into three administrative districts with the Northern District, which contained Butaritari (Makin), Little Makin, Marakei, and Abaiang Atolls. Butaritari is the northernmost of the Gilberts' atolls.

The Japanese presence on Makin

Most Europeans had evacuated the islands before the start of war, but a few remained on Butaritari. On December 9, 1941 the Japanese arrived, and the Europeans were interned by the 300-man Gilberts Invasion Special Landing Force – detached from the 51st Guard Force on Jaluit – which temporally occupied Butaritari, Marakei, and Abaiang. However, they allowed the few French priests to remain. The Japanese soon departed, but returned on December 24 to establish small garrisons that served as outlying guards for the Marshalls. They also briefly occupied Tarawa, 105 miles to the south of Butaritari, on December 10 and 24, rounding up a few Europeans including coast watchers. Seaplane bases were also established for patrol aircraft

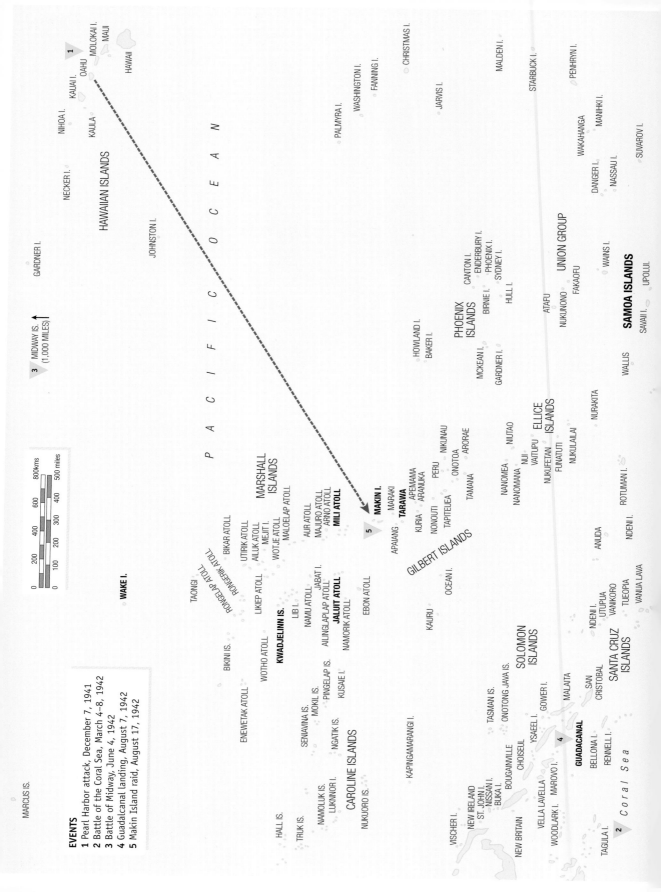

MARCUS IS.

EVENTS

1 Pearl Harbor attack, December 7, 1941
2 Battle of the Coral Sea, March 4–8, 1942
3 Battle of Midway, June 4, 1942
4 Guadalcanal landing, August 7, 1942
5 Makin Island raid, August 17, 1942

0   200   400   600   800kms
0   100   200   300   400   500 miles

WAKE I.

P A C I F I C   O C E A N

HAWAIIAN ISLANDS

MARCUS IS.

MOLOKAI I.
MAUI
HAWAII
OAHU
KAUAI I.
KAULA
NIHOA I.
NECKER I.
GARDNER I.
JOHNSTON I.

CHRISTMAS I.
FANNING I.
WASHINGTON I.
PALMYRA I.
JARVIS I.

MALDEN I.
STARBUCK I.
PENRHYN I.
MANIHIKI I.
WAKAHANGA
DANGER I.
NASSAU I.
SUVAROV I.

3 ◄ MIDWAY IS.
(1,000 MILES)

TAONGI
RONGERIK ATOLL
RONGELAP ATOLL
BIKAR ATOLL
UTIRIK ATOLL
AILUK ATOLL
MEJIT I.
WOTJE ATOLL
MALOELAP ATOLL
AUR ATOLL
MAJURO ATOLL
ARNO ATOLL
MILI ATOLL
BIKINI IS.
WOTHO ATOLL
LIKIEP ATOLL
MARSHALL ISLANDS
LIB I.
NAMU ATOLL
JABAT I.
AILINGLAPLAP ATOLL
JALUIT ATOLL
NAMORIK ATOLL
EBON ATOLL

ENEWETAK ATOLL
KWADJELINN IS.

HALL IS.
TRUK IS.
SENIAVINA IS.
NAMOLUK IS.
LUKNNOR I.
MOKIL IS.
NGATIK IS.
PINGELAP IS.
KUSAIE I.
NUKUORO IS.
CAROLINE ISLANDS
KAPINGAMARANGI I.

KAURU

OCEAN I.

5 ► **MAKIN I.**
MARAKI
TARAWA
APEMAMA
ARANUKA
KURIA
APAIANG
NONOUTI
TAPITEUEA
PERU
NIKUNAU
ONOTOA
ARORAE
TAMANA
GILBERT ISLANDS

HOWLAND I.
BAKER I.
PHOENIX ISLANDS
CANTON I.
ENDERBURY I.
BIRNIE I.
PHOENIX I.
SYDNEY I.
MCKEAN I.
GARDNER I.
HULL I.

ATAFU
UNION GROUP
NUKUNONO
FAKAOFU

WALLIS
NURAKITA
SAMOA ISLANDS
SAVAII I.
UPOLUI.
WAINS I.

NANOMEA
NANOMANA
NIUTAO
NUI
NIUTAO
VAITUPU
NUKUFETAN
FUNATUTI
NUKULAILAI
ELLICE ISLANDS

ROTUMAN I.
ANUDA
NDENI I.

VISCHER I.
NEW IRELAND
ST. JOHN I.
NISSAN I.
BUKA I.
BOUGAINVILLE
CHOISEUL
TASMAN IS.
ONOTONG JAVA IS.
SOLOMON ISLANDS
YSAEEL I.
GOWER I.
VELLA LAVELLA
MAROVO I.
WOODLARK I.
NEW BRITAIN
TAGULA I.

2 ►
Coral Sea

BELLONA I.
RENNELL I.
4 ► **GUADACANAL**
MALAITA
SAN CRISTOBAL
UTUPUA
VANIKORO
TUEOPIA
VANUA LAVA
SANTA CRUZ ISLANDS
NDENI I.

NAMES AND PRONUNCIATION

For clarity's sake the names of the islands and atoll must be discussed. The August 1942 Marine raid is universally referred to as the Makin raid. Officially the Gilbert Islands atoll is Butaritari (pronounced "Pu-tari-tari") but it is commonly referred to as Makin (properly pronounced "Muc-kin," but pronounced "Maken" by Americans). Butaritari and Makin were used interchangeably in official documents for both the atoll and its main island, which was the objective. In the 19th century it was known to Europeans as Touching Atoll. Its Allied codename was *Kourbash*. The Gilbert Islands were codenamed *Overfed*, and the Japanese called them Girubato Shoto. The native name for the Gilberts is Kiribati, pronounced "Ki-ri-bas." Little Makin Island (Makin Meang, or North Makin) is 4 miles to the north of the Butaritari Atoll's northeast corner. The objective island in this work, the southern and westernmost of Butaritari Atoll's islands, will be referred to as Makin.

reconnoitering to the south and east. These operations were launched by the 4th Fleet. By the summer of 1942 they felt there was little threat from the Americans far to the south, and they reduced the already-small garrisons.

The Japanese on Butaritari Atoll established a small seaplane base along with radio and weather stations; the latter were not mentioned in Marine documents. The Japanese base on Makin had a minor military role. It was a way-station for flying-boat patrol-bombers that flew down from Kwajalein. The crews could refuel there, tinker with the engines, and rest. They patrolled the vast ocean approaches from the south and southeast. Allied-occupied New Caledonia, Fiji, and Samoa were far to the south, and to the east were the American-occupied Howland, Baker, and Phoenix Islands. Arriving back at Makin, they could radio their reports to their main base before flying home.

The 6th Base Force on Kwajalein was responsible for service support, and the 6th Defense Force operated coast artillery and antiaircraft guns and controlled the three guard forces distributed throughout the islands. The IJN air units were subordinate to the 22nd Air Flotilla headquartered on Roi-Namur. The IJN personnel on Butaritari were from that command as well as the 51st Guard Force. It was redesignated the 61st Guard Force during the summer, before the raid.

A target for the Raiders

In summer 1942 Admiral Chester Nimitz, commanding the Pacific Fleet, directed the study of several possible objectives that the 2nd Raider Bn could strike in mid-August. The raid was to serve as a diversion for the Guadalcanal landing scheduled for August 7, which the 1st Raider Bn was participating in, but as assault troops only. By raiding a small objective with the 2nd Bn ten days after the Guadalcanal landing, it was thought to be effective timing to disrupt possible Japanese reinforcement efforts. They might commit troop reinforcements and air and naval assets to the diversion target instead of Guadalcanal or delay the Guadalcanal reinforcement in expectation of further action in the vicinity of the raid's objective.

Possible targets were Attu Island in the Aleutians off Alaska (occupied by the Japanese as a diversion during the June battle of Midway), railroad

Opposite:
The Central Pacific theater of operations. The Gilbert Islands are just to the west of the International Date Line – if it is August 17 in the Gilberts it is August 16 in Hawaii. However, even though west of the International Date Line, Hawaii time zone dates were used by US forces conducting the Makin raid.

tunnels on Honshu (the main Home Island), a coastal steel mill on Hokkaido (the second largest of the Home Islands), Tinian Island off Saipan in the Mandate, Wake Island (captured in December 1941), and Makin Island in the Gilberts. Another possibility was a raid on Tulagi, close to Guadalcanal, *prior* to the main Guadalcanal landing. Its goal would be to destroy the floatplanes based there before the invasion fleet arrived.

Carlson was summoned to Pearl Harbor in late March to take part in the study and to develop the initial plan. During the study the above targets were gradually rejected. Attu off the southwest coast of Alaska was far too distant; it was closer to Russia than to Guadalcanal and weather could be problematic. It was considered mainly because it was occupied American territory and a strike there would boost morale at home. A pinprick attack in the Home Islands, especially on Honshu near Tokyo, would have a great effect on morale and inflict a bitter psychological blow to Japan. But it was much too far away (4,000 miles), heavily patrolled, and pursuit was assured when the Raiders withdrew.

Like Attu, Tinian was deemed too far from Guadalcanal (2,000 miles) to have any effect on reinforcements. The Japanese in the Marianas had sufficient resources to deal with a small raid. Wake Island, which also would have provided a high morale boost, was likewise too remote to affect the reinforcement of Guadalcanal. Beginning in February 1942, the US had commenced making Wake Island nearly untenable by shelling and bombing, leading to it becoming virtually cut off. The Japanese would probably not make much effort to reinforce Wake. A pre-invasion raid on heavily defended Tulagi would only alert the Japanese on nearby Guadalcanal.

Makin was selected because it was defended by a small force of mostly non-combatants, which two Raider companies could overwhelm with little difficulty. It was also close to a main Japanese bastion in the Marshalls to the north. This would demonstrate that the US had the ability to strike into Japanese-controlled territory. It might deflect reinforcements destined for Guadalcanal to the Gilberts, plus perhaps convince the Japanese to retain ships and aircraft in the Marshalls and Gilberts instead of sending them to the Solomons.

Concept of the operation

The comparatively small raiding force was employed owing to the limitations of the two cruiser submarines available for transport. A third cruiser submarine was on-hand, the USS *Narwhal* (SS167), but it was committed to a patrol off Japan. However, it had not departed on that mission until July 7; if it had been deemed necessary, it could have been re-tasked prior to its departure, as the operation had been planned as early as March. It may have been felt that the control and coordination between three submarines necessary for launching three Raider companies in the dark would have been a challenge. As it was, there were significant coordination problems between the two submarines and Raider companies during launch and recovery. The main reason though was that a strength of three Raider companies was deemed unnecessary.

Subsurface transport was the only practical means available. Surface transport deep into Japanese territory would have required a significant escort and would have most likely been discovered during its approach, with subsequent loss of surprise, which was essential. It would certainly have had to fight its way out, suffering casualties and possibly the loss of or damage to ships. Seaplane transport was totally impractical and not even considered.

Little coordination was necessary to launch the Makin operation. It involved only two submarines and no surface vessels or aircraft. The Raiders were already at the launch site, Pearl Harbor. Logistics concerns were limited to what the Raiders carried aboard the submarines. There were few moving parts, no coordination with other forces, no air movements, and no diversions or deception operations by other units. It involved one small ground unit and two submarines on a mission requiring a ten-day approach, one day spent on the objective, and most likely a shorter return voyage. Command-and-control efforts would be minimal, although effective coordination between the submarines and the Raiders was essential. Once the submarines departed they would maintain radio silence. Task Group 7.15, as it was dubbed, was on its own until it returned.

Raiders inflate an LCR(L) on the deck of a destroyer transport in preparation for a practice launch. (Tom Laemlein/Armor Plate Press)

USS *NAUTILUS* (SS-168) (EX-V6)

The *Nautilus* was one of three US cruiser submarines built, the largest US submarines until the nuclear USS *Nautilus* (SSN-571) was launched in 1954. It was launched and commissioned in 1930. Its sister was the USS *Narwhal* (SS-167). These were extremely long-range submarines, with heavy torpedo loads and the unusual deck armament of two 6in/53 Mk XII Mod 2 guns and two .30-cal machine guns. Other US submarines mounted a single 3in or 4in gun. There were four bow and two stern 21in torpedo tubes. In 1940–41 it was modified with two forward and two aft torpedo tubes beneath the new elevated gun deck, plus external storage tubes for eight to 12 torpedoes. At the same time it was re-engined with a pair of more powerful 2,350hp diesels to run the two 1,270hp electric drive motors. The engines and hull were based on World War I German designs. Surfaced displacement was 2,730 long tons, length was 371ft (as long as a

destroyer), and beam was 33ft 3in. It could make 14 knots surfaced and 6.5 knots submerged. Range was 9,380 nautical miles (17,370km) at 10 knots and 25,000 nautical miles (46,000km) at 5.7 knots. Test depth was 300ft (91m). Its complement was eight officers and 88 enlisted men.

The *Nautilus'* first wartime patrol was from May 24 to July 11, to support the coming battle of Midway. It attacked a battleship and carrier, but inflicted no damage owing to misses and defective torpedoes. Enduring numerous depth-charge attacks, it damaged two destroyers, an oil tanker, and a merchantman. Its second patrol was the Makin raid. The *Nautilus* conducted 12 more patrols before being decommissioned in June 1945, before the war was even over, owing to hard use. It was broken up before the year's end.

Aboard the *Nautilus* in Pearl Harbor after the Makin Island raid. Roosevelt is to the left, talking to Cdr Robert A. Haines, the task group commander. Note the 6in gun – a very large-caliber weapon for submarine armament. (NARA)

USS *ARGONAUT* (SM-1) (EX-V4)

The USS *Argonaut* was the first US V-class cruiser submarine and the first and only one built in its class. It was additionally designed as a minelayer (SM), with 60 mines able to be laid via two special stern tubes; there were no stern torpedo tubes. It had four 21in bow tubes, two 6in deck guns, and two .30-cal machine guns. The *Argonaut* was on patrol near Midway Island when Pearl Harbor was attacked, but was unable to attack the Japanese destroyers it had detected. It returned to Pearl Harbor on January 22, 1942 and then proceeded to California for modification. It received new engines and electronic equipment, the complex mine-laying system was removed, and two external torpedo-storage tubes were added. During its modification it received two new 3,175hp diesels to power the two 1,270hp electric motors. Surfaced displacement was 2,710 long tons. Its length was 381ft, and its beam was 33ft 10in. It could make 13.6 knots surfaced and 7.4 knots submerged. Its range was 8,000 nautical miles (15,000km) at 10 knots. Test depth was 300ft (91m), and its complement was eight officers and 78 enlisted men. "SS-166" was the code reserved for it, but back at Pearl Harbor it was quickly converted to a troop-carrying submarine in time for the Makin raid. However, it was not redesignated APS-1 until September 22, after the raid. It was to be transferred to Brisbane, Australia in 1942, and while en route conducted its third wartime patrol, in the New Britain and Bougainville area, where it sank a gunboat.

USS *Argonaut*, photographed shortly after its 1927 completion. (NARA)

On January 10, 1943 it detected a convoy of five merchant ships escorted by three destroyers en route to Rabual. It attacked a destroyer but inflicted no damage. A Japanese seaplane spotted the sub and dropped two depth bombs, and the destroyers attacked with depth changes. A passing US aircraft witnessed the *Argonaut* break the surface and come under fire by the destroyers. It was sunk off the upper east coast of New Britain with the loss of 102 hands, the highest loss of life on a US submarine during the war.

The two cruiser submarines, USS *Nautilus* (SS-168) and USS *Argonaut* (SM-1), comprised Submarine Division 42 of Submarine Squadron 4. Captain John H. Brown, Jr. was the Commander, Submarine Squadron 4, and doubled as Commanding Officer, US Submarine Base, Pearl Harbor. "Task Force 7" was how Commander, Submarines, US Pacific Fleet (under Rear Admiral Robert H. English) was known. The operation was under that command, which answered to Commander, US Pacific Fleet, Admiral Chester W. Nimitz.

The Raiders' immediate tactical mission was to capture prisoners and documents of intelligence value, and destroy facilities, equipment, and supplies. Strategically the mission was to create a diversion, and instill confusion within the Japanese command whose responsibility it would be to marshal forces to counterattack Guadalcanal. It would also discourage further Japanese thrusts to the south. Unknown to the US at the time, the Japanese had already cancelled plans to seize the Samoas, Fiji, and New Caledonia owing to their defeat at Midway. It was also acknowledged that a successful raid, no matter how small in scale, would provide a moral boost at home and a blow to the Japanese high command.

Bluntly put, the results could potentially be extremely beneficial at a low cost. Operation *Watchtower* – the seizure of Guadalcanal – was risky, hastily launched, and poorly supported, with troops dubbing it "Operation *Shoestring*." It needed all the help it could get. The small raiding force was expendable, and its loss would not be disastrous in the bigger picture, although its complete loss or it suffering disproportionate casualties could have an adverse impact on morale and national pride. The operation was also a useful test for the Raiders and the concept of submarine-delivered raids. It was essentially a small scale "test exercise."

It was possible that if the raid had failed it would have been hushed up, at least until the Guadalcanal operation succeeded. The risk of losing a submarine was deemed moderate, certainly less severe than the risk faced by regular patrols, as the submarines were to refrain from attacking enemy ships unless they threatened the Raiders ashore.

The key to the operation's success was the submarines. They had to navigate 2,029 miles with no intervening landmarks to verify their position. Not only would they have to find the needle-sized island in the haystack of the Pacific, but they needed to rendezvous in the dark at a precise time. An unspoken fear of the Raiders was that enemy aircraft and surface ships might drive off the submarines or prevent them from recovering the rubber-boat-borne Raiders, stranding them on the island. The huge cruiser submarines were slow to dive and were unwieldy when submerged, requiring a large turning radius, making it difficult to avoid depth-charge attacks. Being so large, they made a conspicuous target for surface ships' sonar, were easily detected by patrol planes at periscope-depth and even deeper in the clear Pacific waters, and they were slower than their design speed. Conditions on board would be extremely cramped and hot. A 5-ton air conditioner was installed in each submarine, but they were of little help.

THE PLAN

Once Makin was selected as the target, it was realized how little intelligence was available. It was known to be a minor seaplane base and radio station, with considerable supplies stockpiled there. It was suspected that it might be the main Japanese headquarters in the Gilberts. Tarawa to the south was known to have significant activity, but Makin was incorrectly thought to be more important. Construction of Tarawa's airfield, the only one the Japanese built in the Gilberts, did not start until October, after the raid.

In mid-July, Co A and B commenced special training at Barbers Point Naval Air Station, 10 miles southwest of Pearl Harbor. Carlson selected these two companies as they were the first to be organized and had trained

Major James Roosevelt (garrison cap and canteen) with Raiders in training. (US Marine Historical Center)

RAIDER WEAPONS

The Marine Raiders employed a variety of light weapons. Carlson's principles included the requirements that:

1) weapons were able to deliver high rates of fire, as he knew his Raiders would often be outnumbered, as well as to take advantage of the overwhelming shock effect of a high volume of automatic fire;

2) weapons were lightweight and compact, to ease transport in cramped destroyer transports, submarines, and rubber boats, and because he expected lengthy speed marches over rugged jungle terrain;

3) every Raider be able to operate all weapons assigned to the battalion as well as Japanese weapons.

The .30-cal **M1 Garand semi-automatic rifle** (eight-round clip) armed one-third of a rifle squad, plus the squad leader. Other than M1 rifles used by the US Army and Philippine Scouts on Luzon at the start of the war, Makin would see the first use of the M1 in combat, for the Marines on Guadalcanal were still armed with M1903 Springfields. The next day, on the far side of the world, 50 Army Rangers accompanying British Commandos used M1s at Dieppe, France.

The .30-cal **M1918A1 Browning Automatic Rifle** (BAR) (20-round magazine) was heavy, but provided accurate, automatic fire, and its range was farther than that of the M1 rifle. They were not yet issued the new M1918A2. The M1918A1 lacked the A2's butt-support monopod and improved rear sight, and the bipod was attached forward of the handguard, not at the muzzle. It was capable of semi-automatic and full-automatic fire, and not the low and high rates of the M1918A2. Men armed with BARs often removed the bipod to reduce the weight by 2½lb.

The .45-cal **M1928A1 Thompson submachine gun** (20-round magazine) was capable of both full-automatic and semi-automatic fire. Its heavy bullets were ideal for smashing through brush, but their range though dense vegetation was limited.

Private Harry E. Huston after the raid with his M1918A1 BAR. The bipod is removed, as was common practice. Displayed on the bulkhead are a captured Japanese flag and fan. (US Marine Historical Center)

the longest. The officers were briefed on the target. The troops had no idea what their objective was and were told not to speculate about it with anyone, even other Raiders. There was of course a great deal of scuttlebutt suggesting that they were going to recapture Wake Island, the Marianas, perhaps Guam (a seized American possession), or a key Japanese base in the Marshalls.

The Raiders practiced paddling and using the outboards. The motors were unreliable – on some days they worked and the next they would fail to start – and they were easily drowned in the surf. The Raiders all cross-trained on their jobs: boat captains, coxswains, motor mechanics, and paddlers. Men were designated to inflate the boats, mount motors, and fuel them. They would use compressed-air hoses run up the submarines' hatches, but also strenuous hand-pumps. They learned that when launching from the beach, all hands carried the boat, with the taller men forward to drag it into

Right: The "Raider knife" was designed by Marine LtCol Clifford Shuey, based on the British Commandos' Fairbairn-Sykes fighting knife. (Leroy Thompson)

A **three-squad Raider rifle platoon** task-organized for Makin was armed with 14 M1 rifles, nine BARs, and 11 Thompsons, although some NCOs substituted trench guns for M1s – tremendous firepower for 34 men. Carlson's Raiders did not use the inferior .45-cal M50 Reising submachine gun, though they were trained in its use along with the Johnson M1941 rifle and M1942 light machine gun. No .30-cal M1 carbines were available.

The **company weapons platoon** was armed with two 60mm M2 mortars, though these were not taken on the raid. There were also four .30-cal M1919A4 Browning tripod-mounted light machine guns weighing 44lbs each. These had incendiary and tracer ammunition with which to fire upon moored seaplanes.

The **battalion** had a pool of 15 British .55-cal Boys Mk I antitank rifles (five-round magazine). Two of these were taken ashore, mainly for testing their use, even though no tanks were present. They were believed lost in the surf during the withdrawal. Weighing 31lbs the bulky hard-recoiling, bipod-mounted weapons were nicknamed "elephant guns."

Some .30-cal **M1903 Springfield** bolt-action rifles (five-round clip) were used, as were .45-cal **Colt M1911A1** pistols (seven-round magazine), which were carried by officers and most NCOs. Some men carried four spare magazines. A few men had civilian-made .38 and .45 **revolvers**. Some NCOs and perhaps others carried 12-gauge **M1897 Winchester trench guns** (pump-action shotgun, six-round tubular magazine). Large numbers of Mk II "pineapple" **fragmentation grenades** were taken ashore, along with extra crates of small-arms ammunition.

The Raiders used a copy of the British Fairbairn-Sykes fighting knife or "commando knife," a 7⅜in-long stiletto that they called the "**Raider knife.**" The main difference was that the grip was zinc–aluminum alloy instead of brass, in order to conserve supplies of the latter. The alloy, though, deteriorated quickly, which meant that the grip cracked and the guard broke off easily. It had little use as a utility knife. Carlson's battalion later made wide use of the Collins Type 2 survival knife used by the Army Air Corps since 1932, commercially known as the Collins No. 18. Nicknamed the "Gung Ho knife," it had a very wide 9½in Bowie-type blade.[4] However, the Raiders did not receive the 1,000 they purchased until September, which was after the Makin raid.

Most Raiders later replaced the "Raider knife" with "Gung Ho knives" or the Ka-Bar utility/fighting knife. Prior to the issue of the "Raider knife" they were issued the "Western Stiletto," the Western States Cutlery No. L77. It had a 7in spear-type blade and was therefore not a "stiletto." Commercial hunting knives were also used. The 16in blade of the M1905 bayonet was used on M1 and M1903 rifles, and the Raiders were taught to use it in hand-to-hand combat.

4   Often called the "V-44," this is a post-war collector's name.

deeper water with the shorter men aft. They would climb into the boat and begin paddling, after which point the taller men would board.

Behind the Barbers Point beach, simple replicas of the likely Japanese installations on Makin were laid out using white cloth tape. They bore little resemblance to the actual installations, of which little was known, but they only had to be positioned correctly relative to one another and the proper distance from the landing beaches to help the Raiders work out movement timing. They were briefed that the beaches and surf conditions at Barbers Point were similar to Makin's. But seen today, it appears that the beaches were not very similar: the Barbers Point beaches are wider with lava rocks in many areas, and the vegetation is mostly brush and scattered trees. Makin had narrower sand beaches and was a coconut-palm plantation. The offshore bottom conditions and gradient were very different, owing to the significantly

AUGUST 7, 1942

Guadalcanal invasion begins

heavier surf at Makin, and it was made worse by poor seasonal weather. The Raiders noticed in aerial photos of Makin, without knowing the target's name, that the wave lines were very closely spaced, more so than at Barbers Point.

The submarines assigned to the mission were unavailable until just before departure. The *Nautilus* had returned from a patrol on July 11 and was refitting for Makin. The *Argonaut* had returned from San Diego after overhaul and was in the process of converting into a troop transport.

In the meantime, training continued. Two buoys were anchored offshore, and the Raiders would paddle or motor out to them. On a signal, they headed for the target beach in their rubber boats. They did this countless times, day and night, in different surf and wind conditions, in the rain, and at high and low tide. They became proficient and learned not to count on the motors, which had to be cleaned after each practice run. They practiced with full combat equipment, including helmets, but also without clothes and even without paddles in case they lost everything. They first practiced as individual 11-man boat teams, then as platoons, then companies, and finally the entire task unit.

Once they mastered the boats they conducted rehearsals ashore after each landing. In full equipment they carried the boats to the vegetation line and rapidly camouflaged them. The platoons then moved out to their objectives. However, this was of limited benefit owing to the inadequate intelligence. Once on Makin, and in darkness, the Raiders would have to adapt immediately to the situation.

To keep motivation strong, on July 31 Carlson told his Raiders that the raid was "go," but still not what the target island was. They trained hard in preparation for the mission for three weeks and managed a single dress rehearsal launched from the *Nautilus* in the dawn hours of August 7, about the same time 1st MarDiv landed on Tulagi and Guadalcanal – although they did not then know of the landing. The Raiders learned just how cramped and hot the submarines were. Admirals Chester Nimitz and Raymond Spruance watched from shore and were surprised that at night they could not detect the approaching boats until they were just 50ft from the shore. There was a final critique, and the Raiders broke camp to return to Camp Catlin. They were confident and as prepared as they could be, considering the deficiencies in intelligence about their target.

The Raider company and task organization

In 1942 the 801-man 2nd Raider Bn[5] consisted of a 135-man headquarters company with a battalion HQ (including two Navy surgeons and eight corpsmen), a communication platoon, a quartermaster and motor-transport platoon, plus six 111-man companies (A–F). The company HQ had a 20-man combat section (including two corpsmen) that accompanied the unit on operations plus a ten-man supply section, which remained at the base. The two 29-man rifle platoons had a four-man HQ (lieutenant platoon

5   In 1942 the 1st ("Edson's Raiders") and the 2nd Raider Battalions were organized differently, due to their commanders' differing philosophies.

commander, platoon sergeant, sergeant platoon guide/demolition NCO, and messenger). There were two rifle sections led by a sergeant, each section with two ten-man rifle squads. These contained a corporal squad leader and three fire groups,[6] each with a submachine-gun-armed group leader, BAR-man, and rifleman. The 30-man weapons platoon had a five-man HQ, an eight-man mortar section (2×60mm), and two nine-man machine-gun sections (2×M1919A4 each). The machine-gun section consisted of a sergeant section leader and two four-man gun squads.

Because of space limitations on the submarines, both Co A and B reorganized and left behind 25 and 30 men, respectively. A battalion surgeon was attached to each company to form a three-man "medical section." These were Lt Stephen L. Stigler (Co A) and Lt William B. MacCracken (Co B). Most histories state that both companies left behind a "rifle section." In reality both of the companies' platoons left behind one squad and both section leaders, leaving them with three squads per platoon. The weapons platoon left its mortar section, giving the weapons platoon only its commander and two two-gun machine-gun sections. A two-man Boys antitank-rifle section was formed in both company HQs. There was also an eight-man task-unit HQ with four officers and four enlisted men (see box), called a "command group" in most histories.

The *Nautilus* served as the Task Group 7.15 command boat, with Cdr Robert A. Haines commanding Submarine Division 42, Submarine Squadron 4. Submarine division commanders normally did not accompany patrols, but this mission was an exception as both submarines in his division were conducting a joint patrol. The numbers embarked aboard each submarine are disputed in historical sources. A best estimate based on unit muster rosters and the task-unit operations order are that 79 Co B men boarded the *Nautilus* along with six from the command group, including LtCol Carlson and his intelligence officer, 1stLt Gerald Holtom. The "roomier" *Argonaut* loaded 136 Raiders, 106 from Co A and 27 from Co B, along with Maj Roosevelt and the demolition officer, Capt James N. M. Davis. Company A was commanded by 1stLt Merwyn C. Plumley and Co B by Capt Ralph H. Coyte.

The total strength of Task Unit 7.15.3 was 14 officers and 208 enlisted men, for an aggregate of 222, often listed as "221" owing to a math mistake in the operations order.

James Roosevelt was the 2nd Raider Battalion's XO, here (center) photographed as a lieutenant colonel in the 1st Marine Raider Regt after the Makin Island raid. To the right is Col Harry B. Liversedge, commanding the 1st Marine Raider Regt. Roosevelt commanded the regiment's 4th Raider Bn during its training, but would not accompany it into combat owing to health problems. (US Marine Historical Center)

---

6   Incorrectly called "fire teams" – a later term – in most sources.

The Makin raid as planned – Operations Order 1-42

Carlson's operations order as issued on the day of departure from Pearl Harbor is paraphrased here to show the original plan as envisioned. The actual execution ten days later was much altered on the fly. Oddly, the raid was one of the few Pacific operations not assigned an operation codename.

The enemy force on Makin was estimated at 250 troops possibly supported by seaplanes and one or two surface craft. The nearest land-based enemy aircraft were 170 miles to the north (Mili, actually 210 miles away). The nearest enemy-occupied islands were 70 miles south (Abaiang and Marakei). No friendly forces were within supporting distance.

Task Unit 7.15.3, the Raiders, would execute landings on Makin in the early morning of August 17 to kill enemy troops, destroy installations, and capture documents and prisoners. The mission would be completed and the troops withdrawn in the early evening. Other histories mention that Little Makin was to be attacked the next day, but there was no mention of this in the operations order. It is doubtful even whether the Japanese occupied Little Makin.

The submarine rendezvous would be 2.6 miles off the northeast point of the main southern island (Makin) on a bearing of 229 degrees. From that point it was 3 miles to Co A's Beach "Y" and 2 miles to Co B's Beach "Z" on the ocean (south) side. Beach "Y" was opposite On Chong's Wharf and Beach "Z" opposite Government Wharf, which were 3,000yds apart. Those wharves were thought to define the limits of the Japanese-occupied area. In effect, the Raiders would perform a pincer maneuver, attacking from both flanks and from the enemy's supposed rear, as they were oriented to the lagoon side. This double envelopment was a distinctively Japanese maneuver. The Japanese practice, though, was to land further away from the enemy's flanks rather than directly at their flanks.

Carlson chose to land on the ocean side, even with its rougher surf, since intelligence indicated that Japanese defenses were concentrated on the lagoon side between On Chong's and Government Wharves. Additionally, the submarines would not enter the shallow lagoon as they could not dive or maneuver effectively there, making them easy targets for aircraft. The Raiders could have been launched from outside the lagoon's entrance on the atoll's west side, but it was 4–5 miles across the lagoon to the objective area. Even with outboard motors this was a long haul, and the motors could not be relied upon. It also made for a longer and more exposed withdraw route.

After moving to within 500yds of the shore, Co A and the accompanying Co B element would depart the

TASK UNIT 7.15.3 TASK ORGANIZATION

Task Unit Headquarters

Commanding officer	1
Executive officer	1
Intelligence officer	1
Demolition officer	1
Interpreter	1
Radioman/runner	3

Companies A and B

Company Headquarters

Commanding officer	1
Demolition officer	1
Gunnery sergeant	1
Radio operator	2
Runner	3
Demolition man	7
Antitank rifleman	2

1st and 2nd Rifle Platoons

Platoon leader	1
Platoon sergeant	1
Platoon guide/demolitions NCO	1
Radioman/Runner	1

1st, 2nd, and 3rd Rifle Squads

Squad leader	1
Fire-group leader	3
Automatic rifleman	3
Rifleman	3

Weapons Platoon

Platoon leader	1

1st and 2nd Machine-Gun Sections

Section leader	1
Squad leader	2
Machine-gunner	2
Assistant machine-gunner	2
Ammunition bearer	2

Medical Section

Medical officer	1
Corpsman	2

Three LCR(L)s lined up in a column. It was in this formation that the Raiders approached Makin Island's beach. (Tom Laemlein/ Armor Plate Press)

Argonaut at 0240 hours and paddle to the *Nautilus*, arriving at 0255. Company A would depart the *Nautilus* using motors at 0305 and the reunited Co B would depart at 0320. Both companies would land on their respective beaches at 0400. These times were later moved forward an hour.

The company boat formations would form in three columns of three boats connected by ropes plus a tenth boat. On reaching the surf line the boats would cast off, deploy into a single line, and land in unison. The boats would be concealed in the foliage beyond the beach to prevent their detection by aircraft. Both companies would establish a boat guard of at least one fire group.

Company A to the left (west) would land on Beach "Y" and rapidly move northwest across the island to the main lagoon-side road. It would deploy security on its left (southwest) flank and capture the west half of Butaritari Village, including the Burns Philip Store. It would destroy vital installations, with particular attention to On Chong's and King's Wharves. After reaching the Burns Philip Store it would establish contact and maintain liaison with Co B on its right flank (northeast).

Company B would land on Beach "Z" and move northwest across the island to the lagoon-side road, secure its right (northeast) flank, and capture the east half of Butaritari Village, exclusive of the Burns Philip Store.

COMMAND STRUCTURE, MAKIN RAIDING FORCE

Task Group 7.15 SubDiv 42, Subron 4	Cdr Robert A. Haines (*Nautilus*)
Task Unit 7.15.1 USS *Nautilus* (SS-168)	LCdr William H. Brockman, Jr.
Task Unit 7.15.2 USS *Argonaut* (SM-1)	LCdr John R. Pierce
Task Unit 7.15.3 CO, 2d Raider Bn	LtCol Evans F. Carlton (*Nautilus*)
XO, 2d Raider Bn	Maj James Roosevelt (*Argonaut*)
Company A (-)	stLt Merwyn C. Plumley (*Argonaut*)
Company B (-)	Capt Ralph H. Coyte (*Nautilus*)

It would destroy installations with particular attention to Government Wharf and the Japanese Trading Station, and maintain contact with Co A on its left (southwest) flank.

The attack was timed to catch the Japanese when they were still asleep. The two companies were expected to make contact in the vicinity of the church near Stone Pier. The task-unit command post (CP) would land with Co A and remain with Co A until directed by the task-unit CO (Carlson).

The first priority was to destroy the two radio stations, whose exact locations were unknown. Possible locations were On Chong's Wharf, Stone Pier, Government House, and the Japanese Trading Station, but they could be anywhere. As soon as practical, both companies were to destroy any seaplanes in the lagoon with machine guns using incendiary ammunition.

The medical officers would accompany their respective companies with two corpsmen. Company A's aid station would be located at a suitable site near the lagoon side near the company's left flank. Company B's aid station would be similarly located near the company's right flank.

Prisoners were to be sent to the task-unit CP "as early as practical for examination and further disposition." Carlson was opposed to the directive to capture enemy personnel. He was concerned about securing them while engaged and having to secure and guard them in rubber boats returning to the submarines, especially since all hands may have to paddle. In addition, the boats would be crowded, as some were bound to be damaged, and litter casualties required more space than a sitting man. Guarding them on the submarines would also be problematic. Some NCOs told their men not to bother with prisoners. Carlson directed that the natives were not to be harmed.

Communication would be by SCR-536A "handie-talkie." Four radio nets were used: Task Unit Net, Co A Net, Co B Net, and Ship-to-Shore. An element needed a separate radio to talk on each net. The code word "BOSMA" was used to clear the net for the task-unit HQ to make emergency broadcasts. Spare batteries were carried for each radio. Each company carried an Aldis "blinker" lamp to leave with the boats. Aldis-lamp recognition signals (Morse-code blinker) were "RDX" and "KGH." The Raider verbal countersign was the challenge "Hi Raider" followed by the reply "Gung Ho."[7]

Carlson had sole control of the task unit once they departed the submarines. The Navy task-group commander could order Carlson to return to the submarines if it was deemed necessary for them to depart. The Navy commander promised Carlson that they would not depart without making every effort to recover all the Raiders. He also said that if they were forced to depart the immediate area because of enemy air or surface-ship activity they would return as soon as possible. The submarines would not remain surfaced the entire time the Raiders were ashore; they would submerge if aircraft approached. They would also provide on-call fire support with their four 6in guns. Communication could not be made with the submarines when they were submerged.

7　The challenge "Gung" and the reply "Ho" reported in some sources are incorrect.

The planned withdrawal time was 1830 hours, with an alternate time of 2100 if enemy aircraft were present. Withdrawal to the boats would be executed on the order of the task-unit HQ. In the absence of orders the companies would withdraw so as to be prepared to embark at 1830. Either way, the boats were expected to return to the submarines 30 minutes after departing the beach.

One unit of fire (a basic load of ammunition) was specified, but many carried additional ammunition. The Raiders carried a canteen of water and a single 4oz D-ration bar. They carried no bivouac gear or packs, as the intent was to remain on the island for no more than 16 hours. They did carry Mk IVA1 gasmasks, which were mostly discarded.

Japanese dispositions and intelligence

The exact locations and nature of Japanese installations and defenses were unknown. Some US carrier planes had conducted photoreconnaissance over the atoll on February 1, six and a half months prior to the raid. A B-17 bomber photographed the island on July 23, and this was the source of the photo-mosaic used to plan the raid. The densely spaced palms and patchy clouds over the islands effectively hid anything on the ground. It was assumed the Japanese would occupy the Government House at the base of Government Wharf, the Native Hospital, Burns Philip Store, and On Chong's Store. The latter was in fact used by the Japanese as a barracks. There was also a Japanese trading store, but it is not known if this was established in one of the existing stores. It was estimated that the Japanese defenses would be oriented to the lagoon side and concentrated between On Chong's and Government Wharves.

The raid's objective area lay between Stone Pier and Government Wharf. Near the Stone Pier and church was a two-story HQ building north of the church, a barracks, and a small rifle range 300yds south of the church

The Government Native School near Government Wharf in 1943 after the US Army captured Makin. It was used by the Japanese as a barracks and was typical of government-built buildings on the island. (US Marine Historical Center)

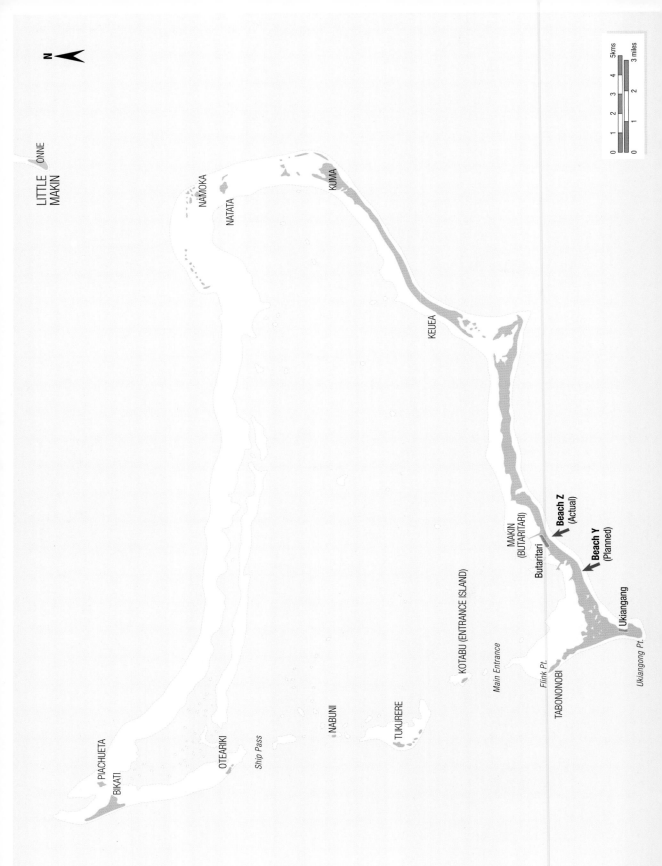

N

LITTLE ONNE
MAKIN

PIACHUETA
BIKATI

OTEARIKI

Ship Pass

NABUNI

TUKURERE

KOTABU (ENTRANCE ISLAND)

Main Entrance

Flink Pt.

TABONONOBI

Ukiangong Pt.

Ukiangang

Beach Y
(Planned)

Butaritari

MAKIN
(BUTARITARI)

Beach Z
(Actual)

KEUEA

KUMA

NATATA

NAMOKA

0 1 2 3 4 5kms
0   1   2   3 miles

THE OBJECTIVE

Butaritari, or Makin, is situated at 3°10' N 172°50' E, 120 miles north of Tarawa, and is the northernmost of the Gilbert Islands. The nearest atoll in the group is Abaiang, 90 miles due south. Kwajalein Atoll in the central Marshalls is 550 miles to the northwest and Truk, which was the main Japanese naval bastion, is in the eastern Carolines, 1,265 miles west-northwest.

The triangular-shaped atoll's southeast side is about 18 miles long and comprised of two long, narrow islands – essentially sandbars. Their maximum elevation is 12ft, with most at a height of 5–6ft. The western and southernmost island was Makin Island, the raid's objective and the atoll's largest island. It is 10 miles long with a 3-mile-long "T" on its west end – a "double peninsula." In the vicinity of the raid's objective area the island is 250–500yds wide. Its east end is in the form of a mile-long hook. Running to the northeast is Kuma Island, connected to Makin at low tide as they are separated by only a half-mile. It is 6¾ miles long and slightly narrower than Makin: 200–350yds. Both are joined by a continuous coral reef that turns north off the northeast end of Kuma for about 4 miles and then, after broadening out, runs west for some 20 miles. Three narrow small-craft passages pierce the north side's reef. There are a few scattered islets on the east end, while the long north side reef is clear of obstacles. At the northwest corner of the atoll is the mile-long wedge-shaped Bikati Island. A limb of the reef reaches 4 miles south along the atoll's west side. It is 10½ miles across the west side between Bikati and Flink Point on the north end of Butaritari's eastern T. The main entrance to the lagoon is on this west side between the little Kotabu Island (aka Entrance Island) and Flink Point. There are two smaller passes on the west side of the atoll, north of the main entrance. Coral heads and shoals are scattered across the lagoon's calm waters.

Little Makin Island (aka Makin Meang) is 4 miles north of Butaritari's east end and is a 7½ mile elongated reef. The main island on the north end is 3⅓ miles long and 1 mile wide, with a few islets scattered in a line off its southern end.

Makin Island is largely covered by coconut palms (which are thicker on the south side), salt-scrub brush, and scattered breadfruit trees. The few open areas are

The lagoon-side crushed-coral road that runs the island's entire length. Coconut palm trees are on the right and breadfruit trees on the left. (Dennis Pack)

covered by low grass. Taro[8] pits of greatly varied size and depth were scattered through the residential areas. The bottoms held a few inches of fresh water. The lagoon side of the north arm of the T, Flink Point, and its junction with the island's long arm is lined with mangrove swamps. Much of the central portion is covered with salt-brush and swamps, except near the shores. The whole of the junction with the T's crossarm is swamp-covered, with interspaced brackish ponds. The eastern portion is covered with palms, thickening toward the east end. A packed-coral motor road ran along the lagoon side of the island's entire length, and almost to the end of the T's southern peninsula, Ukiangong Point, but only halfway up the T's northern peninsula, Flink Point. Just west of the island's center portion was the former British administrative center, which included the Government House, Native Hospital, Post Office, church, and stores. There were four roads crossing the government area connecting to a road running along the ocean side in the island's central area only. The tannish-white sandy beaches, covered in some areas by small coral stones, are 10–20yds wide at high tide on both the ocean and lagoon sides. At the time of the raid, owing to heavy surf and a storm surge, the water was higher. At low tide 300–400yds of the near shore coral flats are exposed. The entire island is bordered by reefs on both sides, 100–200yds across on the southern ocean side and 500–1,500yds wide on the northern lagoon side. Large patches of bottom-growing turtle grass are found on parts of the lagoon reef.

8   A fibrous root with large leaves grown in wet pits and cooked for food.

looking out to sea. Among the buildings were two radio stations. Other than a few machine-gun positions, there was no coast defense or antiaircraft guns and no pillboxes or obstacles emplaced on beaches. Well-camouflaged sniper nests were prepared in palm trees. Other than slit trenches there were no bomb shelters. Makin had only been lightly bombed by aircraft of the USS *Yorktown* (CV-5) on February 1. Makin was assumed to be the Japanese headquarters for the Gilbert Islands or at least the northern Gilberts. Different commands' intelligence staffs estimated anywhere from 50–300 troops on the island. Carlson erred on the high side, with a figure of 250. In reality there were 73 IJN personnel on the island, under Warrant Officer Hisasaburo Kanemitsu (also transliterated as Heisocho Kusaburo). They were detached from the 6th Base Force and 61st Guard Force plus a 22nd Air Flotilla service element. There were no Japanese Army or Special Naval Landing Force troops there. To the Raiders, the Japanese sailors present were simply "Jap soldiers."

The Japanese were armed with Arisaka 6.5mm Miji Type 38 (1905) rifles, Nambu 6.5mm Type 96 (1936) light machine guns, and 5cm Type 89 (1929) grenade dischargers ("knee mortars"). Senior NCOs were armed with Type 95 (1935) swords with a 26.5in blade. All troops carried Meiji Type 30 (1897) 15.75in bayonets even if not armed with a rifle.

No seaplanes were permanently based at Makin, but intelligence thought it possible that some might be present. "One or two surface craft" of unspecified type might have been present in the lagoon. These are usually reported as being a small troop transport and a patrol boat or gunboat, claimed to displace 3,300 and 1,000 tons, respectively. Contemporary film footage during the US Army's November 1943 landing shows two hulks, a steel-hulled trading schooner and a small coastal freighter, both probably used as interisland traders before the war, which were much lighter. The hulks lay 35yds apart in the lagoon, a 100ft-plus craft 270yds north of the lagoon shore and a 150ft craft at 240yds near the fringing reef's edge between On Chong's and King's Wharves. The hulks remain today and are visible at low tide.

Besides the aerial photographs, there were pre-war navigation charts and sketch maps made from the photographs and charts. Only one former resident was located, Lt H.E. Josselyn, Royal Australian Navy Reserve, who provided detailed, but somewhat outdated information to the Raiders. Upon arrival at the island on August 16, the *Nautilus* would conduct a periscope photoreconnaissance from the ocean side. The photographs showed only a low island covered with palms and brush, revealing no military facilities or civilian structures.

THE RAID

At Camp Catlin, Co A and B had supper, packed their equipment and weapons, and were issued D-rations and new field dressings. They placed their black-dyed uniforms, sneakers, helmets, web gear, and toilet kits into gunnysacks and loaded onto trucks after midnight on August 8. The Raiders were quietly trucked to the submarine base adjacent to the Pacific Fleet HQ on the east side of Pearl Harbor, arriving at 0200. They boarded the submarines, their names were checked off, and they lowered their gunnysacks into hatches. Crewmen guided them to their bunks. Most realized that this was the real thing, but some suspected it was just another exercise.

The *Argonaut*'s commander was certain that even with his skeleton crew, the 134 Raiders aboard made this the record number of persons aboard a submarine conducting an offensive mission. All the spare torpedoes were

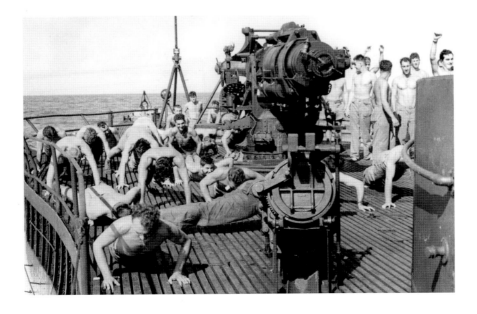

En route to Makin, Company B Raiders enjoy their twice-a-day 10-minute deck-exercise sessions, freeing them from the cramped, claustrophobic, smelly, and hot environment below decks. The device in the foreground is the 6in gun's mechanical time-fuse setter. The gun fired a 100lb projectile. (Tom Laemlein/ Armor Plate Press)

removed from the submarines, leaving only the four in their bow tubes plus the two in *Nautilus'* stern tubes. This provided extra space for passengers, and jury-rigged bunks were fitted in torpedo-rack spaces.

The submarines departed at 0900 and plotted separate winding courses for points southwest of the Gilberts as a deception. The transit would require nine days, and they ran surfaced most of the time. Strict radio silence was maintained, but they could still receive transmissions, and news of the Guadalcanal fighting was piped over the public address system. This buoyed the troops' spirits.

Once on their way, word was passed that this was a real mission, but they still didn't know their destination. The concerned Marines were assured there was sufficient air in the crowded boats, and the smoking lamp remained lit. It was extremely hot and cramped. Sleep was difficult and the boredom seemed unending. The men read, played cards, pilfered canned food stored about the boats, and tried to sleep. It took three and a half hours to serve breakfast and supper. Lunch consisted of soup and crackers, and coffee could be had at any time. Before dawn and after sunset half of the men exercised on deck for 10 minutes, two-dozen Raiders at a time. The submarine had to be able to submerge in three minutes. The brief time spent on deck was much appreciated by the Raiders suffering in the cramped, claustrophobic, smelly, and stifling-hot "pig boats." Marines were detailed to kitchen-police duty, cleaning heads, and other ship's chores.

On August 14 they were within patrol-aircraft range of the Japanese-held islands. The *Nautilus'* radar detected an aircraft and subsequently it remained submerged most of the day. The officers led reviews of each element's plans in small groups.

The Raiders were organized into 11-man boat teams, the odd-numbered teams to launch from port and the even-numbered from starboard. A dry-run rehearsal was conducted on the night of August 14. Not everyone could be on deck in hostile waters, even at night, for it would take too long to clear the decks in an emergency. It was a lengthy process to collect weapons, equipment, motors, and boats from different parts of the submarine and haul it all up through the narrow hatches. Boats were inflated via a compressed-air hose run through the hatch and moved forward. Once in position, equipment was stowed and secured and motors mounted. A total

THE COMBATANTS ON MAKIN

1. The **Raiders** wore a variety of uniforms: black-dyed summer khakis as here, black-dyed utilities, or undyed sage-green utilities. Many, but not all, had makeshift helmet covers made from sage-green utilities. Both sneakers and brown service shoes – "boondockers" – were worn. This man's web gear consists of a pistol belt, suspender, 1-qt canteen, first-aid pouch, and a five-pocket 20-round magazine carrier. A Mk IVA1 gasmask completes his outfit. A third of the Raiders carried Thompson .45-cal M1928A1 submachine guns.

2. This **61st Guard Force (Dai 61 Keibitai)** rifleman is armed with an Arisaka 6.5mm Miji Type 38 (1905) rifle and a Meiji Type 30 (1897) bayonet. He carries two 30-round cartridge boxes and a canteen on his right hip. On the back of his belt is a 60-round reserve cartridge box. Many of the IJA shore-based personnel such as aircraft mechanics, radio operators, supply men, etc, carried only one cartridge box. Such personnel fought the Raiders alongside the guard troops. The dark-green tropical uniform proved to be effective camouflage on Pacific islands, and made it difficult for Raiders to detect snipers.

2027, AUGUST 16

Both submarines arrive on station

The night before the raid Carlson cuts a good luck cake aboard the USS *Nautilus*. The enlisted Raiders in the background wear khaki uniforms of the type that were dyed black for the Makin raid. To Carlson's left is LCdr William H. Brockman, Jr. (commanding USS *Nautilus*) and to his right Cdr Robert A. Haines (commanding SubDiv 42, Subron 4, and Task Unit 7.15 – the Makin raiding force). (US Marine Historical Center)

of 12 boats were aboard the *Argonaut* and eight on the *Nautilus*. The plan was for the submarines to submerge with the loaded boats resting on the deck.

Rendezvous off Makin

Owing to the zigzag courses, rather than traveling 2,000 miles, this distance was almost doubled. The faster *Nautilus* arrived off Little Makin at 0309 on August 16. Turning southwest, it conducted a periscope reconnaissance of Makin throughout the day. No useful intelligence was gained other than observing rain squalls and that the 1½-knot westward tidal current was stronger than expected. Fears that they had struck the wrong island were quelled owing to the relationship of Little Makin to the big atoll.

The *Argonaut* arrived at 2027 the same day. Surfacing in the dark, the wind was blowing toward shore, as was rain. The surf was heavy with whitecaps, and 10ft swells rolled the submarines. The conditions made it dangerous for the rubber boats. That night was the first time the troops learned their objective's name. Commander Haines and LtCol Carlson considered canceling the mission, or waiting a day or two for better weather, but conditions were considered to be barely adequate. Carlson knew that his Raiders were cocked and ready to go up against anything. They decided to execute.

Raiders climbing up the hatch trunk to depart for Makin Island, August 17. The center man wears the V-B rifle-grenade carrier, probably loaded with trench-gun shells. Most of the weapons were tied in bundles and hoisted by rope up through the hatches. They would meet a surging sea and rain once on deck. (Tom Laemlein/Armor Plate Press)

Gung Ho meetings were held on both submarines, with the troops encouraged to ask questions and all available intelligence was provided, what there was of it. They were even told that there might be tanks, air attacks, and ships landing with reinforcements. The Raiders did not care what they faced. They were ready to go and had long had enough of their submarine ride. Carlson had written motivational speeches, which he and Roosevelt read over the public address systems. They reminded the troops they were to wipe out the enemy garrison and destroy everything of use to the enemy. Donning their black uniforms and sneakers (or "boondockers"), they cork-blackened their faces, and prepared their weapons and equipment. The NCOs ensured all weapons were unloaded in order to prevent accidental discharge in the submarines, on deck, and in the boats. The Marines would not load them until they set foot ashore. Supper was ham and mashed potatoes. Before 0200 on August 17 they ate a hasty breakfast, collected up all gear and supplies, and took their stations at the hatch ladders. Hatches were opened at 0330.

Corporal Vernon F. Faulslick, armed with a Thompson M1928A1 submachine gun, passes through a hatch en route to his debarkation station. The weapon's 20-round magazine would not be loaded until he set foot on the beach. (US Marine Historical Center)

In those early morning hours the submarines surfaced to face high winds, driving rain, rolling swells, crashing surf, and a tidal current fighting to pull the submarines toward the coral reef. They had moved to within 500yds of the reef line and ran their engines continuously to hold their position. Lookouts scanned the darkness for enemy ships. The shore could only be made out by the surging white breaker line.

No doubt there were individual concerns, but as a unit they were ready come-what-may. They had trained long and hard and wanted to prove what the Raiders could do and to prove themselves as men. Thoughts ranged from "this will be a piece of cake" to "we're walking into an ambush." Getting out of the "iron coffins" reinforced their enthusiasm.

On the rolling submarines the Raiders struggled to drag the bundled boats out of the external torpedo-storage tubes and to pull weapons, ammunition boxes, medical supplies, litters, fuel cans, and 40lb motors out of the spray-filled hatches. It is a wonder that no one went overboard. No hand-ropes were rigged as the boats needed a clear deck. An improperly connected air hose caused an alarming screech, but the surf's booming crashes covered the sound. Swells increased to 15ft. Men struggled to hang on and to keep their breakfast down.

The boats were inflated one at a time. The Raiders fought to fuel the motors on the rolling, spray-splattered deck; it was almost impossible to keep seawater out. This caused many motors to fail. Gear was tied down, including the 40lb 5gal gas cans needed to refuel the motors ashore. Everything took longer to complete than in rehearsals. It was decided that the boats would have to be lowered over the sides rather than the submarines submerge underneath them. In the swells a submerging submarine would surge up and down, capsizing the boats. A boat with two machine-guns and

RAIDER COMMUNICATIONS

The 1942 SCR-536A, the "handie-talkie," was originally developed for use by paratroopers, but saw widespread use in the infantry. The Marines called it the "spam can" or "walkie-talkie." This 6lb handheld radio had only one pre-set channel and no alternate channel. The earphone and microphone were integral to the radio, and it was turned on and off by extending or closing the 39in telescoping antenna. It required two different batteries, one for the transmitter and one for the receiver. An AM radio, it could not net with any FM radios and with few other AM radios due to its frequency coverage. The only other radio it could talk to was another "536." Its limited utility was aggravated even more by its range of 100ft to 1 mile. It was strictly an intra-company radio, allowing platoon leaders and the company CP to talk to one another. Each company CO had another radio, enabling him to talk to the task-unit CP and other companies. The Raiders communicated with the submarines via "536s" left aboard. The submarines had to be surfaced with the radio on the bridge in order to communicate using these.

ammunition and another with medical supplies were swept away, but spare boats and gear were prepared.

The Raiders had to time their jump into the boats, something for which they had not practiced. A few men missed or bounced off the boats, but all were grabbed and pulled aboard. There were a few minor injuries and weapons and helmets were lost. Hardly any motors started, and the few that did quit exasperatingly soon.

Landing the landing party

All the boats were now loaded and in the surging water. Without any dramatic signal, the *Argonaut*'s 12 boats simply cast off at 0328 and paddled for the *Nautilus*, reaching it at 0334. Its eight boats joined the flotilla. They were all on their way by 0415. Dawn was an hour away.

Carlson and his runner were still aboard the *Nautilus*, so 1stLt Oscar Peatross's (Co B) boat returned and took him aboard with 13 men already in it. Carlson suffered a banged cheekbone leaping in. He was transferred to another boat as Peatross returned to the *Nautilus* twice, once to check for stragglers and again to get pointed on the right bearing, as the other boats had departed. Unable to locate the main body of boats, he headed for shore on his own.

The other boats desperately battled the swells, wind, and current. They were bailing water with their helmets and few of the motors were running. The two intermingled companies were scattered over 100yds and in the darkness it was impossible to identify what boats belonged to which company. Some boats were missing, and it was difficult to take a count in the surging waters and overcast darkness. By now, daylight was approaching. The original plan to land the companies on beaches 3,000yds apart was abandoned. Carlson ordered them all to run to the eastern Beach "Z" and they would sort out the troops there. The orders were passed by voice, amd not all of the boats received the ordered change because of the wind and waves. The rain finally ceased and the wind decreased, but the soaked Raiders were now thoroughly chilled.

As they hit the surf, boats broached (turned sideways to the waves) or capsized, and men were thrown out of others. Weapons and equipment were lost and boats were scattered up and down the beach. Incredibly, no one was lost. In spite of all the hitches, they landed at 0500 as planned on Co B's Beach "Z," more or less. There was still a great deal of confusion, and some men were unarmed. The boats were pulled 30yds to the vegetation line,

0415, AUGUST 17

Raiders paddle for the beach

SGT CLYDE THOMASON, US MARINE CORPS RESERVE

Clyde Thomason (1914–42, born in Atlanta, Georgia) had first enlisted in the Marine Corps in 1934. After serving at Lakehurst Naval Air Station, New Jersey, he transferred to the Marine detachment aboard the USS *Augusta* (CA31), flagship of the Asiatic Fleet, and served in China. He was discharged as a sergeant in 1939. Thomason re-enlisted in January 1942 and immediately volunteered for the Raiders. Being 6ft 4in, he required a height waiver to join Co A, 2nd Raider Battalion. The new battalion departed San Diego for Hawaii in May 1942 and less than four months later arrived off Makin Island.

The Medal of Honor was presented posthumously to Sgt Thomason's mother in January 1943, making him the first enlisted Marine to receive the decoration in World War II. His remains were recovered on Makin in 1999 and re-interned at Arlington National Cemetery, Virginia in 2001. In 1943 the destroyer escort USS *Thomason* (DE203), was named after him. Marine facilities dedicated in Sgt Thomason's name included a gymnasium at Marine Corps Supply Center, Albany, Georgia in 1957; a Staff NCOs' barracks on Marine Corps Base, Camp Smedley D. Butler, Okinawa, Japan in 1984; and the Amphibious Skills Training Facility on Naval Amphibious Base, Coronado, California in 2004. His Medal of Honor citation reads:

(US Marine Historical Center)

"For conspicuous gallantry and intrepidity at the risk of his life above and beyond the call of duty while a member of the Second Marine Raider Battalion in action against the Japanese-held island of Makin on August 17–18, 1942. Landing the advance element of the assault echelon, Sergeant Thomason disposed his men with keen judgment and discrimination and by his exemplary leadership and great personal valor, exhorted them to like fearless efforts. On one occasion, he dauntlessly walked up to a house which concealed an enemy Japanese sniper, forced in the door and shot the man [with a trench gun] before he could resist. Later in the action, while leading an assault on enemy position, he gallantly gave up his life in the service of his country. His courage and loyal devotion to duty in the face of grave peril were in keeping with the finest traditions of the United States Naval Service."

camouflaged, and the troops were told to wait until dawn to reorganize. At 0513 Carlson radioed the *Nautilus* that all Marines were ashore. However, three boats were still missing, with over 30 men. A burst of fire shattered the air when Pvt Vern Mitchell (Co A) accidentally discharged his BAR. Expecting a banzai charge any minute, Carlson radioed "Everything lousy" at 0543. By around 0600 the troops were organized and scouts confirmed that they were on Beach "Z." Carlson then radioed that the situation had improved.

Onto the offensive

One of the three missing boats – Lt Peatross's boat – had landed with its motor operational. Finding themselves alone, they hid their boat. Following the beach to the right, they discovered the two washed-away boats and hid

c. 0600, AUGUST 17

Raiders assemble on the beach

One of the USS *Nautilus'* periscope reconnaissance photographs taken on August 16, the day before the raid. It demonstrates just how low and featureless Makin Island is. The lack of landmarks made it difficult to locate the designated landing beach. (Tom Laemlein/Armor Plate Press)

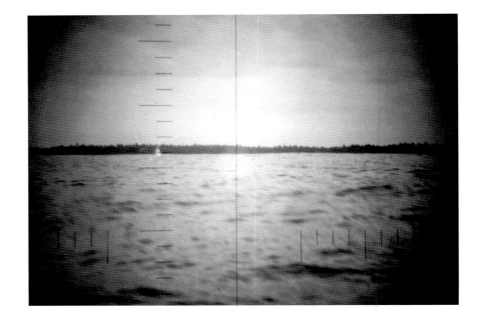

them. They had landed a mile to the southwest of Beach "Z". A Co A boat landed 200yds southwest of Beach "Z" and a Co B boat landed a mile to the northeast. These last two would link up with the main body, but Peatross would not. He moved up the beach and discovered the Japanese rifle range, which he knew was south of the church and Stone Pier. His squad was 1,400yds from the main body of men.

Carlson ordered Co A to advance across the island to the lagoon, even though that had been Co B's mission and Co A was far from its originally assigned zone. Company B would have been more familiar with the objective's layout. They moved into the palms to find that the surf's roar was now muffled, and a thin pre-dawn mist developed. Some Marines were convinced that this was actually an elaborate exercise. A man was dropped off every 50yds to guide Co B forward, as Co B held back to deploy to either flank for security or reinforcement. To confuse matters, some Co B troops had raced ahead toward their objectives. Company A's machine guns and Boys rifle were set up beyond Government House to cover the advance. The benefits of the encircling attack from both Japanese flanks had been lost when the force concentrated on Beach "Z". Company A soon reached the lagoon and identified the bomb-damaged Government Wharf, confirming that they were in the right place.

Three 1st Plat, Co A Raiders approaching Government House were greeted with a blinding blast. After the challenge was made, it turned out to be Co B Raiders who had fired a trench gun at the approaching patrol. No one was hit. The area was devoid of Japanese, and Government House and the wharf were secured. Startled natives appeared and proved friendly. A native police officer had seen the Americans land and had pedaled through the village on his bicycle warning everyone. Some spoke pidgin English, but there were misunderstandings. They told Carlson the Japanese were mostly near On Chong's Wharf 2,000yds to the southwest. The Japanese had been on high alert in the past weeks, ever since the Guadalcanal landing. Conflicting numbers of Japanese were declared, from between 80 and 200. Carlson accepted the higher figure, believing in being prepared for worst-case situations. The Raiders gave the natives cigarettes and D-ration bars and told them to move out of the area for their own safety.

Some men felt that this was turning into a cushy mission. Others were not so certain. There were random shots as Raiders shot at their own scattered men, but no one was hit. The Japanese certainly knew that they were now sharing the island. The haze burned off soon after sunrise, and 2dLt Wilfred LeFrancois's 1st Plat led off in a wedge formation down both sides of the lagoon-side road, towards the Japanese area, and passing beyond the Native Hospital. The lead men inspected every hut and brush clump. Corporal Howard Young was the first to spot the enemy. A truck halted 300yds down the road and up to 20 Japanese piled out. After planting a flag, possibly to mark their position so other troops could rally, they moved into the brush on both sides. More Japanese arrived on foot. The Raider point-men were pulled back and the lead platoon moved onto a low brush-covered rise. Sergeant Clyde Thomason's squad moved into another position as he directed his men into firing positions.

At about 0630 the Japanese advanced in small groups in the fairly open strip between the road and lagoon, their bayonets fixed. LeFrancois swung his left flank inward, creating a fire pocket to trap the unsuspecting Japanese. The rising sun was in the Japanese troops' eyes.

The fight starts

As the Japanese walked into LeFrancois's trap, Sgt Thomason opened fire with his trench gun. The entire platoon then opened up at close range with rifles, Thompsons, and BARs, chopping down most of the enemy. A Boys gunner put a round through the truck's engine. The Japanese returned fire with two machine guns, and their snipers who were amongst the palms. The 2nd Plat moved up and maneuvered to the right. Eventually four machine guns, two grenade dischargers, and a flamethrower (which was never ignited) were knocked out. As the Japanese machine-gunners were killed, the guns would be re-manned. Ten dead were found at an old British Lewis gun.[9] The 1st Plat lost nine dead, mainly to snipers. Things quietened down after 30 minutes, but snipers kept the Raiders pinned down for two hours. It was possible that the Japanese had detected the Raider landing or their advance and were prepared. It would have taken time to emplace well-camouflaged snipers in the tall palms.

Shortly after 0600 Carlson established his CP in a brush clump just off the beach, possibly too far to the rear. He directed 1st Plat, Co B to reinforce the lagoon-side flank. He did not realize that a large portion of the defenders were already dead. The pinned Raiders allowed the remaining Japanese to further prepare by not advancing. Snipers were targeting leaders and radio operators – most of the latter were killed because their shiny antennas

9   Reported as a British Lewis, this may have been a 7.7mm Type 92 (1932) Lewis copy used by the IJN.

THE FIRST DAY

AUGUST 17

The Raiders came ashore in the early dawn hours of August 17 via rubber boats. Most landed in the vicinity of Beach "Z" with the Beach "Y" landing abandoned. A running battle commenced with the defenders, and the Raiders drove off an air-landing reinforcement attempt, downing two aircraft. The effort to withdraw in the evening saw only a small number of Raiders reaching the submarines with the bulk of the force stranded on the island.

▼ EVENTS

1. **0415** Task Unit 7.15.3 departs submarines
2. **0500** Task Unit 7.15.3 lands on Beach "Z"
3. **0515** Lt Peatross lands southwest of main body
4. **0600** Carlson establishes CP
5. **0600** Co A and B moves inland
6. **0630** Co A engages Japanese
7. **0716** USS *Nautilus* fires on and sinks two Japanese ships in lagoon
8. Throughout the day Lt Peatross's squad harasses Japanese rear
9. **1430** Two landing Japanese aircraft shot down by Raiders
10. **1600** Order given to disengage and prepare for withdrawal
11. **1630** Lt Peatross's squad returns to USS *Nautilus*
12. **1930** Prolonged attempt to return to submarines begins. Only 80 men make it
13. **2300** Japanese patrol engaged outside Raider perimeter

■ FACILITIES

1. Government House
2. Native Hospital
3. Radio Station
4. Native Church
5. Barracks
6. Fuel dump

The density of the palm trees has been reduced in order to view the terrain. There were many native huts scattered throughout the area, especially in the Butaritari Village area and to the northeast. Sheds were adjacent to the wharfs and piers along the lagoon-side road.

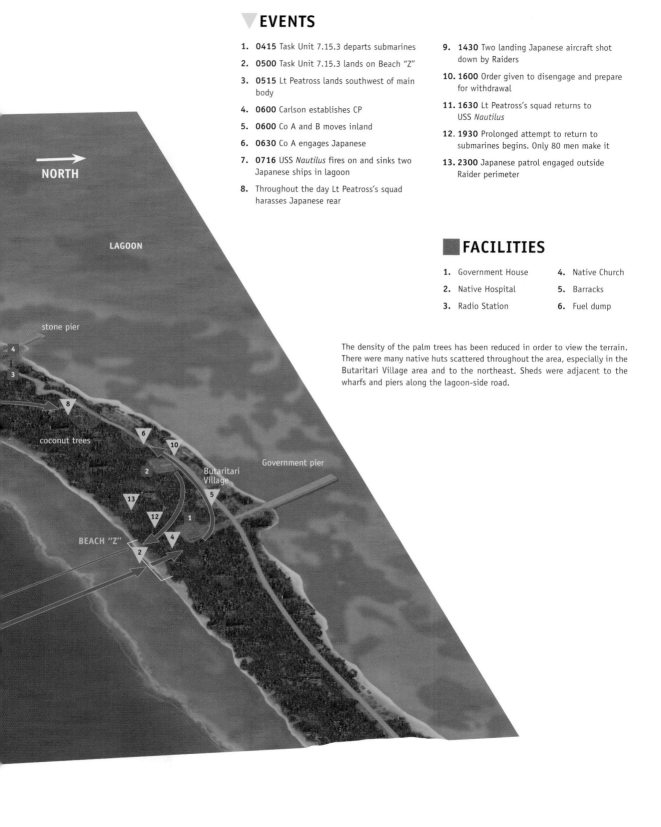

NORTH

LAGOON

stone pier

coconut trees

Butaritari Village

Government pier

BEACH "Z"

attracted attention. Medical personnel ripped off their red-cross armbands. The Raiders had simply not been trained to search the tall trees for snipers. It was during this time that Sgt Thomason was killed while maneuvering his men and directing their fire, trying to instill confidence by exposing himself to enemy fire. Also killed was Capt Gerald Holtom, the intelligence officer.

Raider casualties continued to mount, and Carlson deployed 2nd Plat, Co B to the left flank. Lieutenant Joe Griffith wanted to move his platoon up in column of squads for better control, but Carlson ordered a skirmish line. They became intermingled with Co A, and the surviving Japanese were by now regrouping. The stalemate perhaps occurred as Carlson thought there were many more Japanese than there actually were. He could have attacked the Japanese right flank from his left, but with his companies intermingled, he lost the opportunity. Carlson, observing the Japanese in China, felt they were too rigid, and that an aggressive opponent could outmaneuver them. He failed to follow his own counsel.

The situation dragged on until 1130, when shouts and a bugle were heard. The Japanese rushed the Raider position in what is described as a banzai charge, to be cut down in the barrage of automatic fire. This was the start of the "battle of the Breadfruit Trees," in which six more Raiders were lost. Suffering a head wound, Corp I B Earles became delirious, broke away from the Raiders restraining him, and charged into the enemy, shooting several before he was gunned down.

Around ten Japanese attempted another charge, covered by snipers. They were all killed at close range, and organized resistance evaporated shortly after 1130. There were now only a few snipers facing the two companies and fewer than a dozen Japanese near the Stone Pier.

Already Carlson had won a decisive victory, but he did not know it or act on it. Rather than advancing or dispatching patrols, he kept his forces deployed on line. Regardless of Carlson's combat experience and proven past valor, many felt he had become overcautious to the point of timidity. This may have been due to accepting the natives' report of 200 Japanese and the fact that he had suffered almost two-dozen casualties in a short time. He took no aggressive action, nor did he effectively reorganize his intermingled troops. Snipers still harassed the Raiders as they stalked the remaining Japanese.

Peatross

Isolated a mile to the southwest, Lt Peatross and his 11 men moved cautiously to where they hoped the rest of the Raiders were. Radio silence was to be maintained until fighting began. Peatross heard the accidental shots and attempted to make radio contact, but his handie-talkie was water-damaged. He sent scouts to his rear – southwest – to ensure he was safe from that direction. Finding no Japanese, but able to hear the main battle, he determined that all the enemy was between his squad and the main body of Raiders. He sent two men by different routes to contact Carlson. One was driven back by fire and the other did not return, but unknown to Peatross he had reached Carlson. Carlson welcomed the news of Peatross, but he took no action and did not send a runner back to coordinate with him.

Peatross, in true Raider fashion, viewed the enemy as being trapped between Carlson and his little squad. He advanced. A Japanese ran out of the barracks and was gunned down, and two others were shot as they rode off on bicycles. They crossed the lagoon-side road, approached the empty Japanese headquarters, and searched other buildings. A man exited wearing a pith helmet, and Corp Sam Brown shot him down. It proved to be Warrant Officer Kanemitsu, the island commander.

By now they were only 400yds from the main body of Raiders, but still had no word from Carlson. The 12 men formed a skirmish line and advanced into the Japanese rear. In a short time they killed eight and knocked out a machine-gun nest while losing three dead and two wounded. In the process they knocked out a moving automobile and a radio station, while keeping pressure on the enemy rear. Even though they were just a small force, they no doubt created confusion among the surviving Japanese. They grenaded a Chevrolet truck full of weapons and ammunition that which had Marine Corps markings, and which may have come from Wake or Guam.

Peatross's squad continued to cause havoc over the next few hours, roving around the area, shooting at any Japanese they saw and burning whatever they could. They were by far the most active unit of Raiders on Makin.

At the command post

Throughout the day Carlson ventured to and from the frontline from his CP, assessing the situation and visiting individual Raiders. Roosevelt remained at the CP coordinating between the two companies, sporadically contacting the submarines, and sending ammunition forward. The aid stations were nearby, with numerous wounded stacking up, some of them in serious condition. A few snipers had managed to get behind the lines, and Roosevelt had to return fire. He was nicked on a finger by a bullet (but rejected a Purple Heart).

At 0700 Carlson had contacted the *Nautilus* and directed it to fire on Ukiangong Point, 8,000yds to the southwest, to suppress possible Japanese

Peatross's squad attacks (overleaf)
1stLt Oscar F. Peatross (1st Plat, Co B) landed with 11 men – including a ten-man rifle squad – well to the southwest of the main body of Raiders, with which they would never link up, although they would come within 400yds of them. Determining their location, they advanced toward their comrades, killing three Japanese attempting to flee on bicycles. As they approached a group of huts they intended to search, another Japanese emerged from one, waving as if making an arm signal, and made for a bicycle. As with the other Japanese, they opened up with a withering barrage and cut down Warrant Officer Kanemitsu, the island commander. The rifle squad's lead fire group and its squad leader opened fire on the fleeing Japanese commander with the four most commonly used Raider weapons. The squad leader carried a 12-gauge Winchester M1897 trench gun, its ammunition carried in a World War I V-B rifle-grenade vest – with four rounds in each of the 11 pockets. Some squad leaders carried M1 rifles or Thompsons. Each pocket could also hold two M1 rifle clips. Fire-group leaders carried a .45-cal Thompson M1928A1 submachine gun, usually with six 20-round magazines, though some carried 11 magazines in two five-pocket pouches. The squad leader also carried a No. L77 Western stiletto knife. The automatic rifleman carried a .30-cal M1918A1 BAR with at least nine 20-round magazines. One man carried a .30-cal Garand M1 rifle with 80 rounds in his cartridge belt. Peatross continued to aggressively attack into the Japanese rear until it was time to turn back to their hidden boat and withdraw to the USS *Nautilus*. Their contribution to the raid was to kill over a dozen defenders and to destroy an automobile, a truck, and a radio station, with the loss of three dead and two lightly wounded.

The four-engine Kawanishi H8K1 Type 2 "Emily" flying boat in November 1943. It was shot down by Raider machine guns and antitank rifles while attempting to land in the lagoon. It ended up grounded beside King's Wharf in the background. Stripped of engines and parts, the deteriorating hulk rests there today. (Tom Laemlein/Armor Plate Press)

reinforcements there. The *Argonaut* did not fire as it lacked accurate coordinates, and in any case no Japanese were there.

Soon after discovering the Raiders, the Japanese managed to report the invasion to higher headquarters. The Raiders could see no seaplanes on the lagoon, but there were two small ships. Carlson was concerned that they might contain reinforcements, but it was still only 0700. There was no way they could have arrived from even the nearest islands in such a short time.

At 0710 Roosevelt had requested a fire mission on the ships, which were moored close together, west of On Chong's Wharf. The *Nautilus* lacked precise coordinates and the intervening palm-covered island blinded its radar, but it opened fire at 0716, saturating the general area with 65 6in high-capacity shells. Unbelievably, both ships were hit. Carlson could not be certain if they had landed reinforcements or not. Natives reported that 60 troops were aboard the patrol boat (although in reality there were none). Carlson accepted the accuracy of this report as a possibility, and it appeared to have influenced his actions. He was even less certain now. What happened to the ship crews is a mystery. It is unrealistic to think that all were killed. Some may have come ashore, but there is no mention of them in reports or memoirs.

Air attacks

While the battle of the Breadfruit Trees was reaching its climax, the overall battle entered its second phase with the approaching air threat. At 1130 the Raiders heard aircraft, which materialized as two IJN Nakajima E6N2

Type 95 "Dave" reconnaissance floatplanes[10] that overflew the island; the submarines had already detected them on radar, and had submerged. After circling for 15 minutes, they dropped two small bombs and departed. The bombs hit nothing and it is doubtful whether they saw any Marine activity beneath the palms.

At 1255 the *Nautilus* detected 12 radar contacts barreling in from the north. At 0120 two four-engine Kawanishi H8K1 Type 2 "Emily" flying boats, four Kawanishi E7K1 Type 94 "Alf" reconnaissance floatplanes, four Mitsubishi A6M Type 0 "Zero" or "Archie" fighters, and two more Nakajima E6N2 Type 95 floatplanes blitzed the island, dropping mostly 30kg bombs and strafing for an hour and a quarter. The Raiders sheltered behind palms and in taro pits. The attack rattled the Raiders, but they suffered only a few wounded. Peatross's squad to the southwest attracted much of the enemy attention due to the burning truck they had grenaded. Both submarines remained submerged and would not surface again until two hours before sunset. Since it was about an hour-and-a-half flight down from Jaluit, it was estimated that any aircraft would have to depart the area in time to return home before dark.

Ten of the aircraft returned home, but an "Emily" and a "Dave" broke off and landed 2 miles out in the lagoon. The Japanese air commander erred by not having a couple of aircraft orbit over the lagoon to cover the landing aircraft. Consequently, PlSgt Victor "Transport" Maghakian (Co A) directed three machine guns and the two Boys antitank rifles to set up near King's Wharf. As the aircraft taxied in, the Brownings opened fire with incendiary and tracer ammunition at 1,000yds. The Boys fired only armor-piercing ammunition, but fired up to 20 rounds each. The "Dave" floatplane immediately ignited, but the big flying boat attempted to turn away. "Transport" Maghakian – a legendary "Old China Hand" – directed the fire using binoculars to riddle the "Emily." It briefly lifted off, but caught fire, taxied into the seaplane mooring area, and grounded in flames.

The "Emily" could carry 41 passengers. Native reports of 35 Japanese coming ashore, although unconfirmed, added to Carlson's fear of facing a large force. As with the two boats' crews, it appears that no survivors made it ashore – at least not in any significant number. Raiders on King's Wharf continued to fire on the seaplane beached in the inlet 300yds to the southeast. Its wreckage remains there to this day.

Withdrawal

After the battle of the Breadfruit Trees, Carlson made no efforts to advance and complete the mission. With snipers still in the vicinity the Raiders spent the first afternoon doing little other than conducting a few local patrols, scrounging for food and souvenirs, sheltering when aircraft attacked, and waiting. After wasting these hours, late in the afternoon Carlson began pulling back the Raiders. He was hoping to draw the remaining snipers into a more open area. At around 1600 he left the left flank element in place and

10 All mentioned reconnaissance floatplanes were single-engine biplanes, with two- or three-man crews.

After organized resistance on Makin was crushed, the Raiders spent some time collecting souvenirs. **LEFT** Aboard USS *Nautilus* the Raider at the left wields a trophy Arisaka Type 38 rifle and his .45-cal M1911A1 pistol, which many Raiders carried. Their gear lies on a bunk, on which can be seen a Western No. L77 knife. (US Marine Historical Center) **RIGHT** Raiders compare trophies aboard the USS *Nautilus*. The man to the left holds a Japanese 30-round cartridge case. (US Marine Historical Center)

pulled back the center and right. If the snipers followed they would be taken under fire by the left flank.

At 1630 another wave of planes attacked, bombing part of the area vacated by the Marines. It is not known if the Japanese bombed this area because they thought Marines were still there or by happenstance. Reportedly, some snipers who had stolen into the area were hit by their own bombs. Records do not indicate how many or what types of aircraft attacked. Although they broke off their attack after 30 minutes, the submarines remained underwater during the day and ran further out to sea to prevent aircraft over the island detecting them in the clear offshore waters. Being submerged, they were not in radio contact with Carlson.

It was after this attack that Roosevelt recommended to Carlson to start withdrawing to the beach. He understood that it would require more time than usual in order to get the disorganized troops and the wounded assembled and loaded in the boats. If they were to complete the mission by destroying facilities and supplies, this would require more time and either a complicated return to the submarines in the dark or remaining ashore another night and withdrawing in the morning. Of course there would no doubt be more air attacks during this time, and perhaps ships arriving with reinforcements. After consulting with his officers, Carlson decided to withdraw on schedule, and later reported that he thought the enemy was still strong to his front. Most Raiders and historians are in agreement that the enemy was all but wiped out.

Carlson was still unaware of the havoc Peatross had been causing to the southwest. At 1500, Peatross had also decided to pull back to the beach, and his men began destroying anything of value to the enemy before returning to their boat. They had attempted to signal to Raiders they saw on King's Wharf, but were fired at in reply.

At 1700 a detail was sent to the beach to begin preparing boats and alert all others to begin to break contact and withdraw. The boats were un-camouflaged and the troops moved to the beach. A rearguard was established in the palms. The 14 wounded were carried to boats with one or two in each, the most serious going first. One man had been completely paralyzed for life. The rearguard squad was to remain until the other boats were in the water and on their way. Private Raymond Bauml (Co A) accidently fired his weapon, sending Roosevelt and others ducking for cover.

Chaos on the beach

The withdrawal would begin at 1930 under the cover of darkness and at high tide. The submarines were surfaced and their flashing identity lights visible: *Nautilus* used green, and *Argonaut* used red. Between 1730 and 1930 the unit failed to organize. Men simply formed up on the nearest boat, with roughly ten to a boat. At 1930 the order was given to launch boats on Carlson's command, beginning at the ends and working toward the center. The close-interval waves were pounding in hard and fast.

The last two boats in the center were for Carlson's command group and the rearguard – or so it was thought. Carlson boarded the last boat and failed to order the rearguard to withdraw. Some blame the failure on an unidentified NCO who positioned the squad, but as the commander, Carlson was responsible. The squad itself patiently waited, unaware there was no boat.

The boat teams lifted their boats and waded into the surf. They could already tell that the surf was especially hard and that they were in for a difficult haul. When chest-deep, they clambered aboard. Only a few motors started; the rest paddled. Most made it through the first two or three breakers, but no matter how furiously they paddled, they were getting no further. Swamped boats were washed back onto the beach, and they would resolutely start over. Bailing with helmets was pointless in the crashing waves. The swamped, wallowing boats were too low in the water and weighed too much. No matter how hard they paddled they could not make any headway. Many broached or capsized. A few boats, separated only by a few yards from others, made it through the pounding breakers while those next to them were pushed back, probably from a riptide. Weapons and equipment were lost; even shoes and uniforms. Inoperable motors were jettisoned.

Several men almost drowned. Roosevelt was credited with saving three. There were claims of one man screaming, "Shark!" and disappearing. This may have been Corp James Beecher, listed as missing, whose body was found by the Japanese. The paralyzed man went into the surf on several occasions, but Dr Stigler saved him every time. The other wounded had to be assisted by their boat teams.

Peatross waited on the beach to the southwest, still hoping to hear from Carlson. The squad prepared their boat while Peatross studied the wave sequence. Determining that every fifth wave was the smallest, they dragged the boat into the water, and the motor surprisingly kicked in. Making it

1600, AUGUST 17

Carlson orders Raiders to pull back to beach

1930, AUGUST 17

Raiders attempt to withdraw to submarines; only 80 make it

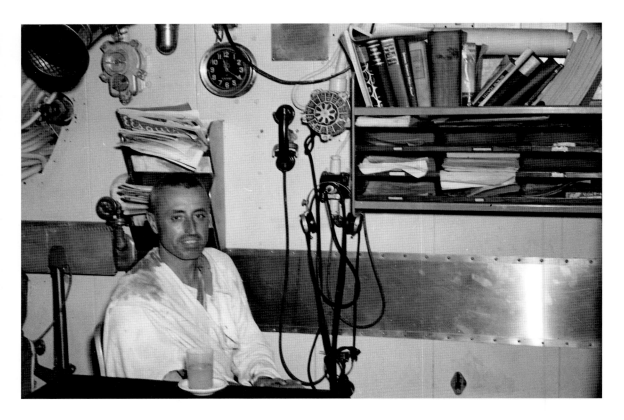

Lieutenant Wilfred S. LeFrancois commanding 1st Plat, Co A rests in the USS *Nautilus*'s wardroom after suffering five 6.5mm machine-gun-bullet hits in his right arm and shoulder during the "battle of the Breadfruit Trees." (US Marine Historical Center)

through the breakers, they headed east in search of a submarine. An hour later they found the *Nautilus* and were the first Raiders to return. Carlson never considered if Peatross knew to withdraw or what his situation was.

Only four boats and 53 men reached the *Nautilus*, and three with 27 men made it to the *Argonaut*. The sailors aboard were shocked at the exhausted Raiders' state, most without weapons, equipment, or even uniforms, and starved.

Stranded

Over the next two or three hours, the rest of the main body's boat teams each made four or five attempts to battle their way through the surf. But, exhausted after a day of close combat with nothing to eat and little to drink, the unsuccessful boat teams were forced to give up. There were concerns now that they would be facing the remaining Japanese or the reinforcements that might arrive the next day without sufficient weapons and ammunition. Physically and mentally drained Raiders, many without weapons and wearing only their underwear, littered the beach as capsized boats washed ashore. Most of the paddles were lost.

Carlson remained on the beach with 120 exhausted Raiders, including most of the wounded. He established a thin defensive line inside the tree line, employing the rearguard squad and the few fit Raiders. There was no shelter from the rain. Perhaps only 30 men were armed, some with only a knife or a grenade or two, others with only pistols. Carlson realized that his men were incapable of making another attempt against the unrelenting surf. They searched for weapons, collected the scattered boats, and did what little they could for the wounded. All hands and boats were moved into the palms, occupying a poor defensive position. It was a long, miserable, cold night. Many feared that the submarines had departed and expected the reinforced Japanese to attack the next day.

It was during that night that the most controversial aspect of the operation emerged. While there is much debate and disagreement among even Marines who were present, it appears that Carlson considered the possibility of surrender. Carlson's morale at this point must have been shattered. His Raiders had not completely accomplished their mission, and he had failed to effectively organize the unit or secure the objective area. He had no idea of how many enemy they were facing and if they had been reinforced – yet certain they would be tomorrow – and more air attacks were expected. He had sporadic contact with the submarines, and while assured they would not leave without them, the fear remained. His troops were exhausted, cold, wet, mostly unarmed, and without food. He had wounded men and little medical support. Carlson was not only concerned for the beached troops, but also had no idea how many had made it to the submarines.

At 2300, eight Japanese approached the covering force. Three were killed by a Raider, who was himself wounded. This reinforced Carlson's fear that the Japanese were far from finished.

The Raiders' dilemma

After midnight, Carlson summoned his officers and senior NCOs for a Gung Ho meeting. It is said that Carlson discussed three options: to fight on regardless of the odds, make another attempt to reach the submarines, or surrender. The word spread through the troops, and they held their own Gung Ho meetings. Carlson visited each group, assessing the men's morale and attitude. It ranged from apprehensive to demoralized. Most though were far from ready to give up. They were willing to try for the submarines at dawn.

Accounts differ, ranging from Carlson calling all hands together and taking a democratic vote, to Carlson consulting only with selected officers, and groups arguing about their course of action. Others claim they never heard any suggestions to surrender until back at Hawaii or on reading accounts after the war. It seems likely that there were arguments and sides were taken within groups. Command authority did not totally break down, but an "every man for himself" attitude lurked. There is little doubt that the subject of surrender was discussed, but the extent of this is debatable.

Carlson had another problem – his XO. Whatever course of action was taken, the fate of Roosevelt had to be considered. Carlson for all practical purposes had promised the President that he would keep him safe, which was a bold promise considering the Raiders' mission. Carlson later admitted he dreaded being summoned to Washington to explain to the commander-in-chief what had happened to his eldest son. Roosevelt's presence was of concern to the troops as well. The consensus was that the country could not afford to allow the Japanese the propaganda coup of capturing Roosevelt and putting him on display in Tokyo. In reality, his presence ruled out the surrender

DID CARLSON ATTEMPT SURRENDER?

According to Lt Peatross (who retired as a major general), at 0330 Carlson *did* attempt to surrender, sending the unarmed Capt Ralph Coyte and Pvt William McCall out to locate the Japanese and give them a surrender note. According to Lt Peatross it read:

Dear Sir,

I am a member of the American forces now on Makin.

We have suffered severe casualties and wish to make an end of the bloodshed and bombings.

We wish to surrender according to the rules of military law and be treated as prisoners of war. We would also like to bury our dead and care for our wounded.

There are approximately 60 of us left. We have all voted to prevent future bloodshed and bombing.

[The signature was illegible.]

According to this account, Coyte found a lone Japanese sailor and gave him the note. They would wait for him to take it to his commander. The doubtless perplexed sailor departed, but was promptly shot down by other Raiders, and Coyte reported his lack of success to Carlson. McCall later backed Peatross's account. The Japanese claim to have found the note and sent it to Tokyo for propaganda purposes, but as far as is known no such note was ever used.

option. Either they had to get him to a submarine, even if it meant leaving others behind, or literally fight to the death.

Roosevelt was apparently kept out of the meetings, and until his dying day he steadfastly refused to comment on details of what was discussed. He claimed that the suggestion to surrender was made by someone other than Carlson, who, being democratic, had presented it as an option, which was widely rejected and the subject then dropped. It would emerge again in the morning.

Yet another quandary faced Carlson: it might not be practical to attempt the submarines at dawn. He knew it would take time, and another air raid was inevitable shortly after dawn. As there would doubtless be multiple raids throughout the day, forcing the submarines out to sea, they would then have to attempt the submarines after dark on August 18 and hope that they were not fighting ship- and air-delivered reinforcements by then. Carlson admitted that this was his "spiritual low point."

On the *Nautilus*, which remained within a mile of shore, Peatross asked to take ten volunteers ashore with weapons and a radio to aid the stranded men. Commander Haines ordered him to wait until they determined the situation at dawn.

DAWN, AUGUST 18

Second withdrawal attempt begins

The second day

At dawn on August 18 Carlson informed the troops that they would cross to the lagoon, take over native canoes along with rubber boats, and make for the lagoon's entrance to the northwest. Any who wanted to attempt to launch in the surf now could do so. The tide was going out and the breakers were diminished. Both submarines backed to the reef, enabling them to rapidly make for deeper water if aircraft appeared.

Two boats made it to the *Nautilus* to relay the situation to Haines. He allowed Peatross to send five volunteers under Sgt Robert Allard (Co B) in a "messenger or rescue boat" to outside the breaker line. They fired a line-throwing gun to shore to anchor them, and a man swam ashore to relay to Carlson that the submarines would be stationed outside the lagoon entrance at 1930.

Two more boats, one with Roosevelt, reached the *Argonaut*. Roosevelt's boat capsized on its first attempt, but made good its second. Carlson had ordered Roosevelt off the island to eliminate one concern. Some Raiders groused that if Roosevelt's safety was so important then he had no business being there to begin with. By 0800 50 men, using rifle butts and palm fronds as paddles, had reached the submarines, just as Japanese aircraft arrived. Carlson had some 30 men stranded ashore, some still unarmed and in bad shape or wounded.

The *Nautilus* was already submerged, but fighters came over the island from the lagoon, strafing the messenger boat and dropping bombs that narrowly missed the *Argonaut* as it dived. Marines ashore thought the *Argonaut* had been sunk and did not see any survivors around the riddled messenger boat – although all did survive. The submarines remained submerged throughout the day some distance away.

Carlson made a new effort to rally the troops, gathering his little band for a Gung Ho meeting. He dispatched patrols to both ends of the island to locate any Japanese and search for separated Raiders. The remainder of the men would move to Government House and search the area for food and water. Some washed-up weapons and uniforms were recovered. The Raiders carried the last four boats with them, dug foxholes near the lagoon, and waited for nightfall. The group could only hope Japanese reinforcements would not arrive, and that they could weather the air attacks.

In the meantime, at 0830 they ignited 1,000 drums of aviation fuel nearby at King's Wharf; destroyed the radio station near On Chong's Wharf; looted the Japanese Trading Station of canned food, biscuit, and beer; and recovered a few documents and charts from the Japanese HQ. In the trading station they even found brightly colored men's silk underwear to clothe Raiders who had lost their uniforms. Natives appeared and provided water and coconuts, and even sarongs to trouserless Marines. The Marines allowed the natives to take what Japanese stores they wanted, bicycles being especially popular. The Raiders' spirits picked up and some hunted for souvenirs.

They patrolled the previous day's battleground, collecting American and Japanese weapons and counting bodies. The count came to 83 Japanese at the Breadfruit Trees battleground and another 30 along the lagoon road. They counted 14 dead Raiders, including the three who had been with Peatross. The five in the messenger boat were presumed dead. Carlson was still not certain if there were others missing, as no firm count was available

Makin Island viewed from the USS *Nautilus* on the morning of August 18. It had run out to sea during the day to avoid detection by aircraft and would return that night to evacuate the Raiders. The men remaining on the island ignited 1,000 drums of aviation fuel near King's Wharf, making it easy for attacking Japanese aircraft to find the island. (US Marine Historical Center)

from the submarines. He gave the native police chief, Joseph Miller, $50 and a few trench guns and cartridges, in payment for burying the American dead after they left.

At 0930 the next Japanese air raid occurred, followed by three more throughout the day, the last being at 1730. Their numbers and types were not reported, as the Raiders hunkered in foxholes could see little through the palms. No casualties were suffered.

They knew they had to get out that night or they might be left behind. With the critical need for submarines and the certainty that Japanese reinforcements were on the way, most likely with destroyers, Haines could not risk his submarines for 30 Marines. The natives told Carlson that the surf on the lagoon side was very light and that the Japanese had no defenses on islets near the entrance.

Escape from Makin

At 1000, Carlson dispatched a three-man patrol to examine a 40ft sloop moored near Stone Pier. They killed a Japanese sailor aboard, but found that the sloop was taking on water. Instead, an outrigger canoe was commandeered and the four rubber boats lashed to its sides. Two outboards were available, and Raiders fervently worked on them during the day.

At 1810 the submarines surfaced and at 1930 arrived at a point three-quarters of a mile off the south beaches. Lookouts swept the darkness for a Raider light signal and for any Japanese vessels. Sergeant Kenneth McCullogh (Co B) shinned up a palm and signaled with a flashlight that they were making for the lagoon's main west entrance at 2300.

Another peculiar incident occurred that evening, when 2dLt Charles Lamb (Co A) found Carlson asleep beside a flag pole as the Raiders prepared to move to the lagoon. Carlson stated he would stay behind alone and organize the natives as guerillas – who had little inclination to do so, were untrained, and there were few Raider weapons to give them. This would have been suicidal, as the Japanese, once experiencing native resistance, would have swept the small island end-to-end and probably murdered everybody. The unconventional Carlson may only have been thinking out loud.

The makeshift craft was assembled and the motors mounted on two rubber boats. The wounded were loaded into the boats and the strongest paddlers seated on the outrigger's sides. With the Raiders holding their collective breath, the motors started and the cumbersome craft started across the lagoon at 2030. Progress was slow, and one motor ran out of fuel. While it was being refueled the craft continued forward, the Raiders driving it forward with paddles and the other motor, and attempting to stay on course by aiming at a star on the horizon. A boat on the starboard side requested permission to cast off and make it on their own, as they feared that the slow-moving craft would miss the rendezvous. Carlson, being democratic about it, granted permission. This was a poor decision, especially since neither their names nor a headcount were taken.

The Raiders made the lagoon entrance at 2200 and spotted the submarines' marker lights. This was a tremendous morale boost, but they still had 2 miles to cover in open water fighting against 6ft swells and wind. Lashings broke in the surge, and had to be repaired as the paddlers tried to keep the craft on course. They arrived at the *Nautilus* at 2308 and searchlights were switched on to help the men aboard drag the exhausted Raiders onto the submarine. Even the beaten-down Raiders who had been picked up the night before were shocked at the new arrivals' condition. Carlson appeared to have aged ten years.

An accurate headcount was still impossible, there being no radio contact between the submarines, and men from both companies were mixed aboard the submarines. Rosters were compiled and every man interviewed about whom he knew was dead or missing. A death had to be confirmed by two Raiders. On the *Nautilus* the five men aboard the strafed messenger boat were unaccounted for. The men who had cast off from the escape craft were assumed to have boarded the *Argonaut*. Carlson reported to Haines that he was satisfied all hands were accounted for, or as certain as he could be without confirmation from *Argonaut*. The submarine commanders set course for Pearl Harbor just before midnight, as the doctors continued to perform what would be hours of surgery on the seriously wounded.

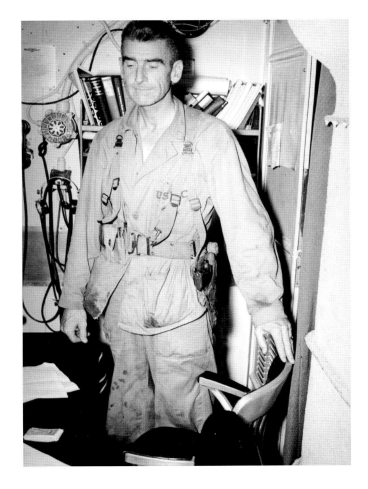

An exhausted LtCol Evans Carlson in the USS *Nautilus* wardroom after making it to the submarine on the night of August 18. (US Marine Historical Center)

THE SECOND DAY

AUGUST 18

In the morning another attempt was made to reach the submarines with only partial success. Part of the force was still stranded on the island and the remaining Raiders endured numerous air attacks. Japanese reinforcements were expected at any time. The Raiders continued to destroy Japanese facilities and material. Finally that night the remaining Raiders were able to withdraw from the island on the lagoon side and rendezvous with the submarines at the lagoon entrance.

OCEAN REEF

Ukiangong
Point

Ukiangong
village

Lagoon Road

freighte
schooner

On Chong's wha

Emily
seapla
wreck

OCEAN REEF

PACIFIC OCEAN

NORTH

▼ EVENTS

1. **0600** Submarines arrive offshore to allow Raiders one more attempt to withdraw and back in toward the reef

2. **0700** Two boats reach each submarine

3. **0800** Messenger boat approaches beach with instructions and is strafed

4. **0830** Raiders set fire to 1,000 fuel drums near King's Wharf

5. **0930** First of three more air attacks throughout the day

6. **1000** 40ft sloop inspected at Stone Pier and found to be taking on water

7. **1900** Raiders move to Government Pier and prepare escape craft

8. **1930** Submarines arrive on station outside of lagoon entrance to northwest

9. **2030** Remaining Raiders depart for lagoon entrance

10. **2308** Escape craft arrives at submarines outside lagoon entrance

■ FACILITIES

1. Government House
2. Native Hospital
3. Radio Station
4. Native Church
5. Barracks
6. Fuel dump

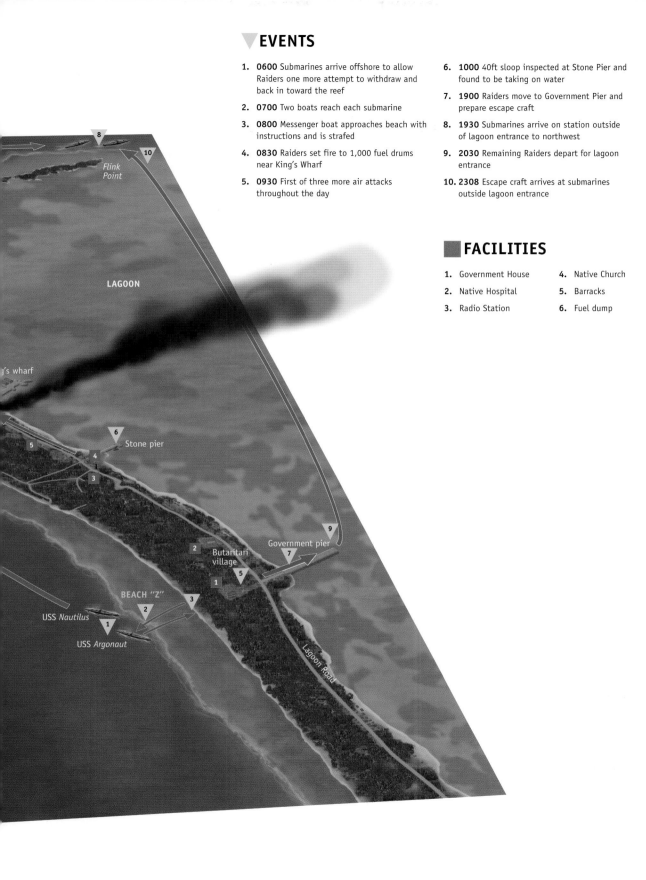

AFTERMATH

A heroes' welcome

The USS *Argonaut* arrives at the submarine base in Pearl Harbor on August 26, a day later than the USS *Nautilus*. Regardless, both submarines and their passengers received the same honors and welcome, complete with Navy and Marine bands. (Tom Laemlein/Armor Plate Press)

As Task Unit 7.15 made its run back to Pearl Harbor, events unfolded on Makin. The island was again bombed the day after the Raiders departed, August 19, and it was not until the next day that several Japanese flying boats delivered troops to secure the battered base area. The following day submarine chasers covered the landing of two rifle and two machine-gun platoons plus two antitank guns. Within two days up to 1,000 troops arrived to sweep the atoll's islands. Their base was quickly reestablished, expanded, and fortified. Surprisingly, there were no reprisals against the natives for aiding the Raiders and taking supplies, but they did demand that the bicycles be returned.

After seven days at sea, the *Nautilus* arrived at Pearl Harbor on August 25. The trip allowed the Raiders to recuperate to a degree, albeit under less-than-ideal conditions. As well as being weakened and exhausted, many were rattled by the failures of their first operation. The haggard Raiders assembled on deck and were astonished to be greeted by the sight of every ship's crew in the harbor mustered at attention in dress uniform, with flags at half-mast. Bands played the "Marines' Hymn" and "Anchors Away." Navy and Marine officers and cheering spectators greeted the Raiders and submariners. The Raiders, unprepared for such a reception, looked slovenly wearing a mix of green utilities, black-dyed outfits, khakis, and borrowed Navy dungarees. The *Argonaut* arrived to the same welcome the next day.

Reeling from their reception, the troops were given the run of the famous Royal Hawaiian Hotel and adjacent Waikiki Beach, an R&R center for submariners returning from patrols. Although promised two weeks' rest, it was cut to one week and they returned to Camp Catlin in order to prepare to move to Espíritu Santo.

On August 25, the day of the Raiders' return to Pearl Harbor, it was publicly announced that the Marines had landed on Guadalcanal and raided Makin. This provided an instant morale boost for the country; the US was finally striking back. Carlson and Roosevelt attended a press conference on August 27, and the press went wild. Articles about the raid and the Raiders appeared in all major magazines and every newspaper ran stories, especially if there were local men involved. The Raiders were completely surprised by this fervor. Being so involved in their training and operations, they did not

Navy and Marines officers greet LtCol Carlson (wearing a garrison cap) aboard the USS *Nautilus*. The khaki-clad Marine officers can be identified by the embroidered braid quatrefoil on the crown of their service caps. (US Marine Historical Center)

DECORATION AWARDEES, MAKIN ISLAND

Medal of Honor

Sgt Clyde Thomason (KIA)	Co A

Navy Cross

Cdr Robert A. Haines (USN)	SubDiv 42, Subron 4
LtCol Evans F. Carlson	HQ
Maj James Roosevelt	HQ
Lt William B. MacCracken (USN)	Co B
Lt Stephen L. Stigler (USN)	Co A
Capt Ralph H. Coyte	Co B
1stLt Oscar F. Peatross	Co B
1stLt Merwyn C. Plumley	Co A
2dLt Charles E. Lamb (WIA)	Co A
2dLt Wilfred S. LeFrancois (WIA)	Co A
GySgt Ellsbury B. Elliott	Co A
GySgt Lawrence A. Lang	Co B
PlSgt Victor J. Maghakian (WIA)	Co A
Sgt Robert V. Allard (MIA)	Co B
Sgt Dallas H. Cook (KIA)	Co B
Sgt James C. O. Faulkner	Co A
Sgt Melvin J. Spotts	Co A
Corp Edward R. Wygal	Co B
PFC Richard N. Orbert (MIA)	Co B
PFC Joseph Sebock	Co A
Pvt Howard R. Craven*	Co A
Pvt John I. Kerns (KIA)	Co B
Pvt Donald R. A. Robertson (MIA)	Co B

* Craven's actual name was William B. Murphree; he had deserted from the Army to join the Marines. The Cross was presented under his real name.

realize just how starved the American people were for any favorable war news. The Navy issued press releases, and anything that could be found about the Raiders was printed, even their "colorful" songs. The numbers of Japanese dead grew to 350. Carlson and Roosevelt were treated as legends, and Carlson's concepts of Gung Ho leadership, often presented out of context, were much publicized. Some Marines were jealous of the publicity garnered by the Raiders, as thousands of Marines were slogging it out half-starved in Guadalcanal's jungle.

In October, Roosevelt briefed his father in person and presented him with a Japanese flag taken on Makin. Carlson, besides promoting his Gung Ho principles, gave assurances that Japanese soldiers could be outwitted and defeated by Americans.

A Medal of Honor and 23 Navy Crosses were presented to the victors of Makin.[11] The submariners presented the Raiders with the Submarine Combat Patrol Pin, a unique honor. However, no matter how much the raid was popularized and its importance to the war effort touted, no Presidential Unit Citation was forthcoming.

After Makin

The battalion departed for Espíritu Santo on September 6, arriving on September 22. They established Camp Gung Ho and their training now incorporated the lessons learned on Makin. They knew they were bound for Guadalcanal. Roosevelt returned to the States in October to raise the new 4th Raider Battalion.

On November 4, 1942, Co C and E led by Carlson landed at Aloa Bay, Guadalcanal in support of an Army force sent to build an airstrip. Two days later they began what became known as the "Long Patrol." They were joined on the 10th by Co B, D, and F, with Co A arriving on the 25th. The Raiders were moved west toward US-held Henderson Field 31 miles distant, through Japanese-occupied territory, harassing the enemy as they went. Resupplied by landing craft and airdrop, they killed almost 500 enemy with a loss of

AUGUST 25 & 26, 1942

Nautilus and *Argonaut* return to Pearl Harbor

11 No Silver or Bronze Stars were presented, the former having just been reinstated and the latter not authorized until 1944.

16 dead and 18 wounded. The Raiders finally closed on Henderson's perimeter on December 4, and the battalion departed for Espíritu Santo on December 15 for rebuilding. Given two weeks' leave in New Zealand, they then returned to Espíritu Santo to resume training.

On April 25, 1943 the 2nd Raiders were shipped to New Caledonia with only 676 troops; meanwhile they had become a component of the 1st Raider Regt on March 15, and LtCol Alan Sharply took over from Carlson on March 22. The 2nd Bn, 1st Raider Regt fought on Bougainville from November 1 to December 15, and on their return to Guadalcanal, the 2nd Bn was deactivated on January 31, 1944. The rest of the Raider battalions were deactivated on February 1 and absorbed into the new 4th Marines, which went on to fight on Guam and Okinawa. The former 2nd Bn troops formed the regiment's weapons company and were scattered throughout the other three battalions. Many of the 2nd Bn troops felt that they had been broken up to ensure that Gung Ho principles were diluted and would not re-emerge.

The Japanese reaction

The Japanese publicly denied the importance of the Makin raid and declared that the "American landing party" was defeated. While the raid failed to divert or delay reinforcements to Guadalcanal, it did cause the Japanese to take the threat of such raids seriously. They improved the defenses and increased the garrisons of many bases in the Gilberts and Marshalls. While this tied down troops and resources, it made the seizing of some of those bases extremely costly for the US the following year. When the reinforced 165th Infantry captured Makin with 6,500 troops 15 months later, they faced 800 Japanese troops, and during the assault just 100 of them were taken prisoner. The Army suffered 224 casualties. When the 2nd

DEAD AND MISSING, MAKIN ISLAND

Killed in action (remains recovered on Makin)

Capt Gerald P. Holtom	HQ
Sgt Clyde Thomason	Co A
Corp Mason O. Yarbrough*	Co B
Corp I B Earles	Co A
Corp Daniel A. Gaston	Co A
Corp Harris J. Johnson	Co A
Corp Kenneth K. Kunkle	Co A
Corp Edward Maciejewski Co A	
Corp Robert B. Pearson	Co A
PFC William A. Gallagher	Co B
PFC Ashley W. Hicks	Co A
PFC Kenneth M. Montgomery*	Co B
PFC Norman W. Mortensen	Co A
PFC John E. Vandenberg	Co A
FM1c Vernon L. Castle*	Co B
Pvt Carlyle O. Larson	Co A
Pvt Robert B. Maulding	Co A
Pvt Franklin M. Nodland	Co A
Pvt Charles A. Selby	Co B

* Member of Lt Peatross's squad.

Missing in action and found dead by Japanese (remains not recovered on Makin)

Corp James W. Beecher (KIA returning to sub)	Co B
Pvt Cletus Smith (KIA ashore)	Co A

Missing in action, captured, and executed on Kwajalein (remains not recovered)

Sgt Robert V. Allard†	Co B
Sgt Dallas H. Cook†	Co B
Corp James Gifford‡	HQ
PFC Richard E. Davis	Co A
PFC Richard N. Olbert†	HQ
PFC William E. Pallesen	Co B
PFC John I. Kerns†	Co B
PFC Alden C. Mattison	Co A
PFC Donald R. A. Roberton†	HQ

† Messenger boat party.
‡ Also listed as Joseph Gifford.

Carlson visits his son, 1stLt Evans C. Carlson, Jr, on Guadalcanal. After the Makin raid, Carlson's son quietly joined the 2nd Raider Bn in command of 1st Plat, Co E. He retired as a colonel and aviator. (US Marine Historical Center)

MarDiv assaulted Tarawa to the south at the same time, it was a different matter: the 17,500 Marines virtually wiped out the 4,800-man garrison, but at high cost of over 3,300 Marine casualties, with over 1,000 of them killed.

The Makin raid is often attributed as the reason Tarawa was so heavily fortified and was taken at such a high cost, but it is debatable if the raid should bear the sole blame for the extensive reinforcement of Tarawa. The Japanese began constructing an airfield there in October 1942, and as it was the only airfield in the Gilberts, it is inevitable that they would have heavily defended such an exposed base.

The missing

The Japanese reported that of their 73 personnel on Makin, they found 43 dead and 27 survivors (some wounded), with three missing. They did not mention casualties from the two ships and two aircraft, which must have been reported separately. The Japanese dead were cremated. The Raiders lost 19 dead, 11 missing,[12] and 16 wounded, and all of the dead were left on the island. As the Japanese reported finding "21 bodies, 5 rubber boats, 15 machine-guns, 3 rifles, 24 automatic rifles, and 350 grenades" the Raiders may have double-counted some bodies. Considering translation differences

12 Carlson reported 18, but 19 were buried by natives along with a native executed for murder by the Japanese. The Japanese found two dead Raiders themselves, which they buried in a different site to the 19.

Roosevelt in California during the training of the 4th Raider Bn, after the Makin raid. (US Marine Historical Center)

in specifying categories of weapons, and Japanese nomenclature practices, the weapons listed probably equate to 15 BARs, three Garand M1 rifles, and 24 Thompson submachine guns. Many more weapons were lost in the surf, some of which were intentionally discarded during the withdrawals. The large number of grenades were no doubt abandoned 53lb cases containing 25 grenades apiece. It is quite possible they were used by the Makin defenders when the US Army landed 15 months later.

No known effort was made to take a complete muster until both submarines had returned to Pearl Harbor. Simply put, it was not known who all the missing were or how they became separated. The fate of the missing Raiders was not known until after the war. The five seen in the strafed messenger boat were reported missing and presumed dead, as were seven more that were thought to have drowned in the attempt to make it through the surf on the evening of August 17. Two of those were found by the Japanese and one by the natives – the 19th man.

It is now known that the five in the messenger boat survived and must have come ashore east of the main body. Four more were somehow separated,

EVANS CARLSON AFTER MAKIN

It was not all honor and glory for Carlson, as there were some commanders who were less than pleased with the results, albeit not uttered in public. At all echelons the raid was publicized as a momentously successful victory, but as after-action reports worked their way through the chain of command, there was disappointment in the raid's results; there was no apparent diversion or delay of reinforcements for Guadalcanal. It was also realized just how small and insignificant an outpost Makin was. Japanese losses were two aircraft, two small auxiliary craft, 1,000 drums of fuel, and maybe over 100 personnel. It was of little military importance. The few recovered documents proved to be of little value and the charts were nothing more than Japanese reprints of US charts given to Japan years before.

Nimitz was extremely displeased with Carlson's draft report, as it mentioned the consideration of surrender. He directed Carlson to remove that section, but Carlson refused. As far as he was concerned, it had occurred so should be included. When the report was passed through command channels, along with the submariner Cdr Haines's report, there was a great deal of dissatisfaction. But as the Makin raid had been valuable as a morale-booster, criticism was kept internal. Commanders at all echelons were split on whether or not similar submarine-delivered raids should be executed.

Carlson was presented with his second and third Navy Crosses, for Makin and the "Long Patrol," and served very briefly as the executive officer of 1st Raider Regt. Carlson was disliked by many officers owing to his outspokenness, unorthodox views, and independence, and he never commanded troops again, holding only staff positions until his retirement in 1946. Ill with malaria, jaundice, and exhaustion, he convalesced in San Diego. After rejecting an OSS assignment, he served as the technical advisor for the movie *Gung Ho!* Back on duty, he was assigned as the new 4th MarDiv D-5 (plans officer) and accompanied the 2nd MarDiv as an observer to Tarawa in November 1943. After the battle of Tarawa he married Peggy Whyte.

Carlson was again the division's plans officer for the highly successful February 1944 Roi-Numar assault, and again for the Saipan assault in June, where he was wounded and later received the Legion of Merit. In March 1945 he was promoted to colonel and again sent to the Pacific as Deputy Chief of Staff of V Amphibious Corps. He then returned home in June for further surgery, and undertook speaking tours.

He was disappointed to never again command troops, and bitter over the rejection of his leadership concepts. Ailing, exhausted, and demoralized, he retired on July 1, 1946, after being promoted to brigadier general. Carlson succumbed to heart failure in Portland, Oregon on May 27, 1947 and is buried in Arlington National Cemetery. While condemned for his offbeat ideas, independence, and the questionable aspects of the Makin raid, few disagreed that he was an exceptional planner, possessed an inventive mind, did not want for valor, and was a firm believer in the Corps.

Carlson's decorations

- Navy Cross (three)
- Legion of Merit
- Purple Heart (two)
- Navy Presidential Unit Citation with three service stars
- Marine Corps Expeditionary Medal
- World War I Victory Medal with France clasp
- Yangtze Service Medal
- Second Nicaraguan Campaign Medal
- China Service Medal
- American Defense Service Medal

possibly during the night or morning attempts to reach the submarines. Why they did not return to the main body is unknown. They may have thought the Raiders and submarines had departed or had been overrun by the Japanese. Nor is it known how the nine linked up. Natives reported seeing some of them and provided them with food and drink.

Regardless, the nine found each other and made their way to Little Makin, where a French priest, Father Clivaz, gave them an outrigger so they could try to escape across the impossible 2,000 miles to Hawaii. He saw them picked up by a Japanese ship after they set out on August 24.

They were shipped to Kwajalein on August 30, arriving on September 2. They were not reported as prisoners to the International Red Cross. In 1946, Navy investigators searching for information regarding two US bomber crews executed on Kwajalein discovered from a native witness that nine "US soldiers"

- American Campaign Medal
- Asiatic-Pacific Campaign Medal with three service stars
- World War II Victory Medal
- Italian *Croce al Merito di Guerra*
- Nicaraguan *Orden Presidencial al Mérito*
- Nicaraguan *Medalla de Distinción* (two)

Lieutenant Colonel Carlson posing with his Raiders after completing the November 1942 "Long Patrol" on Guadalcanal. They display captured Japanese Nambu 6.5mm Type 96 (1936) light machine guns, which they also faced on Makin Island. (US Marine Historical Center)

had been executed in the fall of 1942. This came as a surprise, and the island commander during that time was located in Japan and arrested. He was Vice Admiral Koso Abe, who had been informed in October 1942 that no ship could be sent for the prisoners. He subsequently ordered their execution. On October 16, 1942 they had been taken to the southwest end of Kwajalein, beheaded, and buried in a pit. Admiral Abe confessed to ordering the execution and he, Capt Yoshio Obara (61st Guard Unit CO), and LCdr Hisakichi Naiki (Obara's XO) were tried on Guam in 1946. Abe was hanged in 1947. Obara and Naiki were sentenced to ten and four years, respectively. Obara was released after five years and Naiki served his full sentence.

In 1948, an unsuccessful effort was made by the American Battle Monument Commission to locate the Raiders' remains on Makin. In 1999 another attempt was made by the US Army Central Identification Laboratory,

Navy and Marine officers greet the raiders aboard the USS *Argonaut*. Major James Roosevelt can be seen beside the torpedo-loading davit wearing a garrison cap. Note that the Raiders to the extreme left wear a black-dyed khaki shirt, Navy dungarees, and the Raiders' sneakers that many wore on the raid. (US Marine Historical Center)

Hawaii, in which the 19 Raiders buried by natives were located and returned home. The two buried by the Japanese were not found. In 2002, CILHI searched for the remains of the nine Raiders murdered on Kwajalein, but the end of the island had been greatly altered by heavy bombardment, storms, and landfill. Nothing was found.

A memorial plaque for the nine murdered Raiders was emplaced on Kwajalein in 2002. The original plaque was replaced the following year by another that omitted the controversial words "left behind." Today Butaritari Atoll, along with all the Gilbert, Line, and Phoenix Islands, are part of the Republic of Kiribati, which was granted independence by Great Britain in 1979.

ANALYSIS

This modest assessment attempts to avoid using hindsight unfairly, and instead looks at the fundamentals of special operations and tactical operations in general that were violated or ignored during the Makin raid.

Rather than the ten Co A boats and two Co B boats launching from the *Argonaut*, paddling to the *Nautilus* together, and becoming hopelessly intermingled with the eight Co B boats at the *Nautilus*, the Co A boats should have departed straight for their beach, which was further away if they had stayed with the original plan. The two Co B boats should have remaining behind and then paddled to the *Nautilus* and join their company.

To change the landing plan at night when already in the boats was a major mistake, especially when the order was not relayed to all boats. Even with the decision not to land Co A to the west as planned, separation of the two units could have been achieved by ordering Co A to swing right far enough to avoid intermingling.

Carlson's inability – or at least the apparent lack of efforts – to assemble, reorganize, and account for all personnel in a mere six platoons after landing is inexcusable. There appears to have been no assembly plan or designated assembly areas for the platoons. Colored flashlights could have been used. Granted, there was confusion and darkness, but this should have been rehearsed. It was never effectively accomplished within all elements even over two days, even though there was slack time after most of the fighting was over and between air attacks.

This negligence is also evident in the officers' failure to record the names of the five men sent toward shore in the messenger boat. The same applied to the men who had cast off from the outrigger. Not even their numbers were known. No one recalled a single man who was aboard and it was simply assumed they made it to the *Argonaut*. No complete muster was undertaken until both submarines had returned to Pearl Harbor.

Once both companies were ashore, the most serious mistake was to order Co A forward rather than sending Co B, which was originally tasked with the mission and had rehearsed for the Beach "Z" area. As it was, some Co B elements rushed ahead of Co A – indicating a lack of control by leaders – and further intermingled with Co A groping its way forward. This could have been, and almost was, fatal, with friendlies firing on one another.

The most serious shortfall was Carlson's lack of aggressiveness after most of the Japanese had been destroyed in the battle of the Breadfruit Trees. Aggressive patrols and probing attacks should have been launched when resistance dwindled – both parallel with the lagoon road and to the left flank. Snipers should not allow a unit to become immobilized. They could have been flanked to the left as another element provided suppressive fire. As it was, key parts of the mission were not accomplished and the destruction caused could have been greater. If the Raiders had withdrawn to the submarines on the first night as planned, little would have been destroyed. When efforts were finally made on the second morning to destroy facilities and materiel, only 30 Raiders were still ashore and some were wounded or otherwise incapacitated.

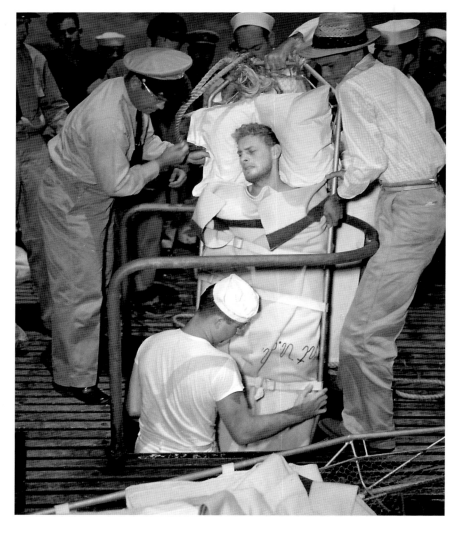

A severely wounded Raider is painfully hoisted out of the USS *Nautilus* strapped into a Stokes litter (adopted in 1907). (US Marine Historical Center)

Another mistake was to carry only one canteen and one D-ration bar under the assumption they would be on the island less than a day. Local safe water and food sources should never be counted on. Two canteens, one meal of C-rations (two cans), and two D-ration bars at a minimum should have been carried.

Surviving Raiders are to this day deeply divided over the question of surrender talk. Some say Carlson presented it as an option. Others say it never arose while still others say Carlson consulted no one, making the decision on his own. Peatross's account suggests that Carlson did in fact try to surrender.

Those denying that Carlson would make such a proposal may genuinely not have heard of the discussion, which is difficult to believe owing to its gravity, or may be protecting Carlson out of loyalty. Not all officers and NCOs were completely accepting of Carlson's radical ideas and, some felt that traditional Marine leadership principles were superior. They went along with it as they believed in the Raiders and because he was their commander. Post8war memoirs written by some officers were practically critical of Carlson's leadership methods, his failures on Makin, and the surrender issue, but none questioned his bravery or dedication.

One benefit of the raid was the verification of the effectiveness of the three-fire-group squad. After Makin and before being committed to Guadalcanal, Raider rifle platoons were reorganized from four squads to three, and the two section leaders eliminated. Ten-man squads retained three three-man fire groups. This was due to reduced strength and the high loss of NCOs at Makin (12 were lost). Additionally, the section organization proved cumbersome and only added an unnecessary layer of leaders between the platoon and squad leaders. In early 1944 the 13-man rifle squad with three four-man fire teams was adopted Corps-wide, and remains in use to this day.

CONCLUSION

Returned Raiders. The M1928A1 Thompson-armed man to the left wears a khaki shirt and cutoff utilities while the other wears black-dyed khakis. He is holding a carton of Camel cigarettes, which could be purchased in a commissary for 50 cents. (Tom Laemlein/ Armor Plate Press)

The raid was hailed as a valorous exploit that greatly upset Japanese plans. There is little doubt that the troops gave their best effort under exceedingly difficult circumstances, but Carlson's leadership was found wanting in this instance. The mission's goals were questionable and the long-term Japanese response was not adequately considered. It is true that no Japanese reinforcements were ever deployed to Guadalcanal from the Marshall Islands, but this was not because of the raid; a different command was responsible for the Solomons area than the Marshalls and Gilberts, and such a reinforcement was not part of the Japanese plan. As a result of the raid,

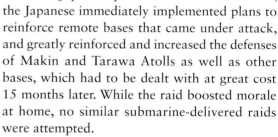

the Japanese immediately implemented plans to reinforce remote bases that came under attack, and greatly reinforced and increased the defenses of Makin and Tarawa Atolls as well as other bases, which had to be dealt with at great cost 15 months later. While the raid boosted morale at home, no similar submarine-delivered raids were attempted.

That said, many reconnaissance missions were subsequently submarine-delivered. Additionally, the USS *Barb* (SS220), after bombarding six Japanese coastal towns on Karafuto Island north of the Home Islands with 5in rockets, landed an eight-man party that emplaced a demolition charge to destroy a train on July 24/25, 1945. But regardless of the problems, errors, and marginal results of the raid, the valor, dedication, and perseverance of the Marine Raiders on Makin Island cannot be faulted. Much can be learned – and was – from this pioneering operation.

BIBLIOGRAPHY

Blankfort, Michael. *The Big Yankee: The Life of Carlson of the Raiders.* Boston: Little, Brown and Company, 1947.

Hoffman, Jon T. *From Makin to Bougainville: Marine Raiders in the Pacific War.* Washington, DC: Marine Corps Historical Center, 1995.

Moran, Jim. *U.S. Marine Corps Uniforms and Equipment in World War 2.* London: Windrow & Greene, 1992.

Peatross, Oscar F. *Bless 'em All: The Raider Marines of World War II.* Irvine, CA: Review Publications, 1995.

Rosenquist, R. G., Sexton, Martin Jr., and Buerlein, Robert A. *Our Kind of War: Illustrated Saga of the US Marine Raiders of World War II.* Richmond, VA: American Historical Foundation, 1990.

Rottman, Gordon L. *U.S. Marine Corps World War II Order of Battle.* Westport, CT: Greenwood Publishing, 2002.

Rottman, Gordon L. *World War II Pacific Island Guide: A Geo-Military Study.* Westport, CT: Greenwood Publishing, 2001.

Smith, George W. *Carlson's Raid: The Daring Assault on Makin.* New York: Berkley Books, 2001.

Updegraph, Charles W. *US Marine Corps Special Units of World War II.* Washington, DC: USMC History and Museums Division, 1977.

Wiles, Tripp. *Forgotten Raiders of '42: Fate of the Marines Left Behind on Makin.* Washington, DC: Potomac Books, 2007.

Wukovits, John. *American Commando: Evans Carlson, His WWII Raiders, and America's First Special Forces Mission.* New York: New American Library, 2009.

INDEX